ROUSSEAU
KANT
GOETHE

TWO ESSAYS

By Ernst Cassirer

TRANSLATED FROM THE GERMAN
BY JAMES GUTMANN, PAUL OSKAR KRISTELLER, AND
JOHN HERMAN RANDALL, JR.

PRINCETON
PRINCETON UNIVERSITY PRESS

To the memory

of my young friend

INGEBORG MÜLLER-RIEMER

February 14, 1908–September 20, 1938

CONTENTS

INTRODUCTION

BY PETER GAY

ASSIRER'S two essays on Rousseau, Kant, and Goethe are large in everything but size. Read sympathetically, and with an eye to current interpretations of the eighteenth-century mind, they are immensely enlightening, both in what they say and what they imply. The Enlightenment has long been hounded by misreadings, and two of the most persistent have been the assertions that the *philosophes* were a narrow, tight group of French men of letters with few real intellectual connections abroad, and that their doctrinaire radicalism was in sharp conflict with other prominent currents of thought, including German Classicism. Ernst Cassirer's two essays confront these two misreadings directly. The first, "Kant and Rousseau," illuminates the cosmopolitan range of the Enlightenment by laying bare the connections between two very dissimilar figures. The second, "Goethe and the Kantian Philosophy," explores the expansion of the Enlightenment in another direction: *Aufklärung* and Classicism appear not as antitheses but as complementary intellectual forces. These are the two explicit themes of this book: for Kant, Rousseau was the Newton of the moral world; for Goethe, Kant was the supreme philosopher of form and experience.

These two manifest arguments, important as they are, build upon implicit meanings which are even more important. To see Kant as a pivotal figure of the Enlightenment is, first, to take it seriously, and secondly, to treat it as a school of thought devoted to empiricism. To do this is to challenge prevailing views of the Enlightenment. If there are two things the average educated man is willing to say about the Enlightenment, it is that it was frivolous and abstract. Probably the most influential, and the most damaging remark made about the *philosophes* in recent years was made by Alfred North Whitehead in *Science and the Modern World:* "*Les philosophes,*" he wrote, "were not philosophers." Whitehead meant well by the Enlightenment: he admired the *philosophes'* clearheaded criticism of prevailing beliefs and institutions, as well as their humanitarian passion for the victims of superstition and ignorance. But he thought them too negative to provide a really satisfying basis for civilization. And the *philosophes* have in general been treated not merely as unphilosophical, but as impractical too. Again and again we hear that the *philosophes* were cynical nihilists, or (on the contrary) that they were fanatical Utopians, but cynic or fanatic, they have usually been denied the capacity for realistic, practical thought.

In his magisterial *Philosophy of the Enlightenment,* and in these two essays which Cassirer hoped the reader would take as an introduction to the larger work, Cassirer reduces these two criticisms to their true dimensions: they stand before us as prejudices rather than justified charges. Instead, the Enlightenment appears as a genuinely philosophical and genuinely empiricist movement, living in the world of affairs and the world of ideas with equal ease. Much becomes clearer as a result of this revaluation, including the *philosophes'* disdain for what they liked to call "metaphysics," a word that became for them a general *Schimpfwort* stigmatizing abstract, rationalistic thinking. The *philosophes,* then, appear as active social philosophers who treated right thinking as a precondition for right action.

All this is pure gain. But Cassirer's essays do more:

they reveal much about the three individual thinkers, especially about Rousseau. Cassirer was fascinated by Rousseau, and returned to him over and over again.[1] While his Rousseau holds few surprises for the specialists (who have read Cassirer's essays on him and made his interpretation a prominent part of their thinking) he is probably new to most readers. For, just as the Enlightenment as a whole has been victimized by persistant misunderstandings, Rousseau has been the target of the most surprising charges. Rousseau the anarchist, Rousseau the father of collectivist totalitarianism, Rousseau the confused aimless dreamer, Rousseau the vicious sentimentalist—these are the popular Rousseaus. Cassirer knew better. He knew that Rousseau had never used the phrase "noble savage" and had never invited mankind to return to its primal innocence. He knew that Rousseau's political thought was neither a demand for defiance of all law or (as others have argued) for total slavish subjection to the state. For Cassirer, Rousseau was a rational philosopher, the roots of whose thought were deeply buried in his complex character and his varied experience, and whose ideas display a consistent development and rest on a consistent principle. The reader of the recent literature will realize that this is the best current understanding of Rousseau, and that it represents a triumph for Cassirer's writings.

There is a special poignancy to Cassirer's love for Rousseau, which finds expression in this little book: Cassirer came to Rousseau through Kant, and began by seeing Rousseau through Kant's eyes. Kant, as Cassirer proudly insists, was probably the first and certainly the most distinguished eighteenth-century reader of Rousseau who admired him for his real, instead of his alleged virtues.

[1] See *The Question of Jean-Jacques Rousseau,* edited and translated with an Introduction by Peter Gay (1954).

For Kant (and for Cassirer after him) Rousseau wanted man to return to his true nature, which was not a simian primitivism, but a genuine cultivation of his highest capacities.

This pregnant reading of Rousseau has its perils, and some of Cassirer's most generous critics have pointed to them.[2] As a Neo-Kantian, Cassirer was apt to see the Enlightenment in rather too orderly a fashion. He found the materialist strand, best exemplified by Holbach and his circle, a minor and unrepresentative mood, rather than a vigorous school in the Enlightenment. And he saw the thought of the eighteenth century leading gradually but definitely toward Kant, who became not only the greatest but also the most typical of the *philosophes*. Associated with this neat view of the century was a Kantian reading of Rousseau: the very real differences between the two thinkers were minimized in Cassirer's writings on Rousseau in the 1930s.

On this point, the present essay on Rousseau is less open to objection than Cassirer's earlier work. Here, Cassirer explicitly distinguishes Rousseau's optimism from Kant's cultural ideal which excludes happiness and is solely directed toward human freedom. "Rousseau was destined by fate to the very syncretism" that Kant condemns. "He set up a strict and lofty ideal of virtue, but he demanded, as the price of serving it, the fulfillment of his yearning for happiness. . . . Kant no longer believes that civilization, even in its highest perfection, can bring about the happiness of mankind, and he no longer asks it to. For him civilization has another law peculiar to itself. It is not the source of happiness, and its meaning does not even consist in providing men with intellectual satisfactions. It is rather

[2] Among them, the most notable is Robert Derathé, in his *Le rationalisme de Jean-Jacques Rousseau* (1948).

the setting in which man is to test and prove his freedom." [3]
This is an important distinction, and one that does justice
not only to one of the most remarkable intellectual filiations
of the eighteenth century, but also to the gulf between the
rediscoverer of nature and the critical philosopher. In his
cultural ideal, Kant stands not with Rousseau but with
Goethe; the poetic philosopher of energetic effort, human
limitations, and artistic form.

This brings me to the essay on Goethe and Kant. Here
the problem is rather different for the interpreter, since
there can be no doubt about the fundamental intellectual
disparity between the two writers. Cassirer recognizes
these differences, and specifies them in some lucid pages.
But he also sees one convergence, a convergence that is of
the greatest importance not only for the Enlightenment,
but for a modern philosophy of culture in general. As
Cassirer reminds us, the rebels of the *Sturm und Drang*
had criticized the *philosophes* for what they called their
rigid materialism. These Germans wanted not discipline
but self-expression, not form but freedom. The young
Goethe agreed with them, and denounced Holbach and his
materialist allies for what he considered a systematic
assault on life. But as he grew as a man and matured as
an artist, Goethe discovered that the question of artistic
freedom did not permit any easy solutions. The rejection
of form in the name of genius, he came to see, led not to
masterpieces but to unsatisfactory fragments.

It was at this point that Kant's Critical philosophy con-
verged with Goethe's poetical experience. In his *Critique
of Judgment,* Goethe found the justification for his own
procedure, his firm reliance on his own inner talent shaped
by what Cassirer calls "the will to form."[4] Kant in philo-

[3] See below, p. 42.
[4] See below, p. 89.

[xiii]

sophical theory, and Goethe in literary practice discovered that form and freedom, far from being mortal enemies, were indispensable if often uneasy allies.

Cassirer's essays are so suggestive that they make us wish for yet a third, an essay on Goethe and Rousseau. Cassirer did not write it, but in his spirit and with his method, we may guess at what he might have said. Goethe was a faithful admirer of Rousseau's, very much as Kant was all his life. And very much like Kant, Goethe knew that Rousseau's writings had been widely, and maliciously, misunderstood. In *Dichtung und Wahrheit,* for example, Goethe inveighs against the modish primitivism of his time, and holds responsible, not Rousseau, but "misunderstood suggestions" of Rousseau's.[5] Goethe, the Classicist, could see the classicism of Rousseau behind the fervent rhetoric.

There was something else that brought the two men together: a morbid subjectivity which they tried to overcome by energetically attaching themselves to external nature. Mercurial in their moods, easily depressed and easily exalted, both Goethe and Rousseau were called "chameleon" by their contemporaries. And in his *Italienische Reise,* Goethe made this odd entry in his journal: "I sometimes think of Rousseau and his hypochondriacal distress; and yet I can understand how so fine an organization can be disarranged. If I didn't take such an interest in natural matters, and if I didn't see that in the midst of apparent confusion one may compare and give order to a hundred observations (as the surveyor verifies a large number of individual measurements with one straight

[5] *Dichtung und Wahrheit, Gedenkausgabe,* ed. Ernst Beutler, 24 vols. (1949), X, 363.

line), I should often think myself mad." [6] The reminiscence is moving, for while Goethe succeeded in rescuing himself from his subjectivity by his interest in science coupled with a relatively healthy psychological organization, Rousseau's attempts to reach inner stability either by self-examination, or by attaching himself to nature by long walks or by botanizing, were a tragic failure. The differences between Rousseau and Goethe, then, like the differences between Rousseau and Kant, remain as important as the affinities. But the affinities open vistas of an international movement of intellect and sensibilities far larger, and far more interesting, than all too many textbooks allow us to see. It is the signal merit of these two essays to have opened them for us.

Columbia University
October, 1962

[6] *Italienische Reise, Gedenkausgabe,* XI, 231. This passage is used by Jean Starobinski, *Jean-Jacques Rousseau: La transparence et l'obstacle* (1957), 291–292.

PREFACE

The two essays in this little book deal with different subjects, but they have a common theme. They try to illustrate, from various perspectives, the culture of the eighteenth century and the "climate of opinion," to use the term of Whitehead, from which this culture arose. I have treated this subject in more detail in my book *Die Philosophie der Aufklärung*. As I am preparing a new and revised English edition of this work which will appear in the near future, I hope that these essays may be read as a sort of introduction to the larger volume. I avail myself of this opportunity to express my gratitude to the editors and Trustees of Princeton University Press who decided to publish this English edition under the present difficult circumstances.

I have to thank Professor John H. Randall, Jr., for his suggestion to present these two essays in the series of monographs edited by the *Journal of the History of Ideas*. I feel especially indebted to James Gutmann, Paul O. Kristeller, and John H. Randall, Jr., for their excellent translation.

ERNST CASSIRER

Columbia University
October 1944

KANT AND ROUSSEAU

I. PERSONAL INFLUENCE

KANT's biographers tell us that his study, which was furnished with Spartan simplicity and lacked all decoration, had but a single ornament—on a wall hung the portrait of Jean-Jacques Rousseau. In other ways also the earliest accounts of Kant's life give varied evidence of his reverence for Rousseau as a person and his admiration for his work. Most familiar is the story that he who was a model of punctuality, and accustomed to regulate his daily routine by the clock, departed only once from this regular routine. When Rousseau's *Émile* appeared, fascinated by the study of the work in which he had become absorbed, Kant gave up his daily walk.

But we do not require the evidence of such stories to convince us of Rousseau's profound influence on Kant. His own authentic testimony is much clearer and much more impressive. It leaves no doubt that what Kant thought he owed Rousseau was not any particular doctrine. Rather, at a crucial turning-point in his development Rousseau showed him the course he never thereafter abandoned. Kant regarded Rousseau not as the founder of a new "system" but as the thinker who possessed a new conception of the nature and function of philosophy, of its vocation and dignity. "I am myself by inclination a seeker after truth," he wrote at forty. "I feel a consuming thirst for knowledge and a restless passion to advance in it, as well as satisfaction in every forward step. There was a time when I thought that this alone could constitute the honor of mankind, and I despised the common man who knows nothing. Rousseau set me right. This blind prejudice vanished; I learned to respect human nature, and I should consider myself far more useless than the ordinary working-man if I did not believe that this view could give worth to all others to establish the rights of man."[1]

At first glance it seems strange and paradoxical enough that Rousseau was able to bring about such a change of heart in Kant. For what could bridge the gap between these two personalities? Was there any immediate kinship between them, or did they not rather form an extreme contrast in character and disposition, in destiny and mode of life? If we examine carefully the personal and philosophic development of Rousseau and Kant, we shall search in vain for any point of contact between the two. They belong to quite different worlds. "The kind of philosophy a man chooses," runs a well known utterance of Fichte's, "depends upon the kind of man he is. For a philosophic system is no piece of dead furniture one can acquire and discard at will. It is animated with the spirit of the man who possesses it."[2] Were this dictum to be applied strictly and universally, it would be hard to discover any kinship between Rousseau and Kant; for in the entire range of the history of philosophy we can hardly find two spirits so little in tune with each other.

A glance at the outward course of their lives and development will suffice to bring into clearest focus this contrast between their two natures. In Kant rule and method constituted the animating and inspiring principles, and they gradually acquired such power that they not only mastered his life in its fullness and variety, but seemed almost to obliterate that concrete fullness. Rousseau tried in vain to subject his life to any rule or to organize it in accordance with any plan. He moved constantly from one extreme to

[1] *Fragments* (ed. Hartenstein, Bd. VIII), 624.
[2] Fichte, *First Introduction to the Science of Knowledge, Sämtliche Werke,* I, 434.

the other, and in the end life eluded him in contradictory impulses. Rousseau never felt completely at home in any profession, in any science or doctrine, in any religion. He practiced in succession the callings of engraver, domestic servant, tax collector and official, tutor, music copyist, diplomatic secretary, musical performer and composer, before he found his true vocation as thinker and writer. Brought up in the strict principles of Calvinism, at the first opportunity he renounced Calvinism for Catholic doctrine; but he abandoned this in turn when in 1754 he returned to his birthplace, Geneva. His life was filled with unsettled wandering, interrupted only in his youth by the quiet and peaceful years spent at Les Charmettes.

Rousseau himself saw this as his destiny; and this destiny was not only forced upon him from without, as when he was driven from place to place during the last period of his life; it expressed and derived from a fundamental trait of his nature, as he felt and admitted. In the *Confessions* he speaks of that inner turmoil of his whole being that forced him to flee from Parisian society. "If the revolution had only restored me to myself, and had stopped there," he adds, "all would have been well; but unfortunately it went further, and carried me quickly to the other extreme. Henceforth my troubled soul crossed and recrossed the line of repose; and its ever-renewed oscillations have never allowed it to remain at rest there."[8]

Rousseau's life could find no point of rest or security, because even apart from external threats there was no point of equilibrium at which his personality could abide. What he achieved he could accomplish only at highest tension and in utter convulsion of his whole being. Only a few of his works, like the *Émile* and the *Social Contract*, ripened slowly in his mind. All the rest are the expression of

[8] *Confessions,* IX, 317.

a spiritual or intellectual crisis which took place suddenly, and unexpectedly overwhelmed him. He has himself described in incomparable and unforgettable fashion the crises that precipitated his first *Discourse* and the *New Héloise*. And ever and again after such experiences he had to start his life and work anew and rebuild them, as it were, out of nothing. There was no prevision to guide him and to protect and shield him from himself and from all the irrational powers to which he felt himself exposed. Over and over, as we survey the course of his life, we are reminded of Faust's words:

> Bin ich der Flüchtling nicht, der Unbehauste,
> Der Unmensch ohne Zweck und Ruh,
> Der wie ein Wassersturz von Fels zu Felsen brauste,
> Begierig wütend nach dem Abgrund zu?[4]

Rousseau is constantly aspiring toward lofty goals, the very loftiest; but he feels that he cannot attain them, and he sees the chasm at his feet, close by and threatening.

If we put Kant's manner of life alongside this of Rousseau's we at once find a marked contrast. Order and law, coherence and consistency, are the guiding stars of Kant's being. We know how he carried this consistency even into small matters, indeed into apparent trivialities. For each and every matter he formulated an appropriate "maxim" and held to it with unswerving tenacity. Some of the circumstances Kant's earliest biographers carefully and conscientiously relate are so strange and extraordinary that we can hardly avoid smiling at them. And yet they ex-

---

[4] I am the fugitive, all houseless roaming,
The monster without aim or rest,
That like a cataract, down rocks and gorges foaming,
Leaps, maddened, into the abyss's breast!
—*Faust*, Bayard Taylor tr., Modern Library,
New York, p. 128.

pressed the whole deep seriousness of his nature. This seriousness kept him from leaving anything in the conduct of life, however unimportant it might appear, to the dominion of chance. The will must prove itself in its independence, in its original autonomy, and take the reins from chance.

This same trait characterizes Kant's career as thinker and writer. From the outset he kept in view a specific goal and determined on an appropriate route. In his first published work he wrote: "I have already traced the course I want to follow. I shall set forth on my way and nothing shall keep me from holding to it."[5] And he acted in accordance with these words spoken at the age of twenty. To be sure, his thought matured very slowly and did not escape crucial upheavals. He himself reports various aspects of the "upsets" his thought underwent in the course of the years. But none of this gainsays the methodical progress of Kant's thought or takes away any of its strictly methodical character. For all the difficulties Kant the "critical" thinker finds within the faculty of reason, indeed all the antinomies he there discovers, enable him only to penetrate more deeply into the structure of reason and to work out its plan and architectonic order more and more precisely. For him, reason is of and through its own powers certain of its own inherent logic. In this logic reason possesses once and for all its surest guiding star, which it can trust at every step in the realm of experience, in the general philosophy of nature, and in the special doctrine of man, "philosophical anthropology."

If we can thus find no immediate kinship between Kant and Rousseau, either with regard to personality and way of life, or with regard to the manner and form of their thought, the question arises as to the nature of the tie that

[5] *Werke*, I, 8.

nevertheless bound them to one another. We know that Kant not only prized Rousseau's style, but that this was exactly what led him to turn again and again to Rousseau's writings. It could hardly be otherwise. For in just that period of his life in which he felt Rousseau's influence, Kant had not yet become the pure analyst concerned merely with the "dry dissection of concepts." He was equally a stylist and a psychological essayist, and in this respect he established a new standard for the German philosophical literature of the eighteenth century. His *Observations on the Feeling of the Beautiful and the Sublime* display a precision of observation and a lucidity and facility of presentation Kant never again attained in any later work. At this time he must have possessed a sensitive ear for Rousseau's distinctive literary style. But he was not disposed to surrender to the magic that Rousseau as a man of letters exercised upon him; he rather struggled against it and tried to substitute for it a calm and tranquil judgment. "I must read Rousseau," he says, "until his beauty of expression no longer distracts me at all, and only then can I survey him with reason."[6]

. Thus Kant seeks neither stimulus nor emotion in Rousseau's writings; it is rather an intellectual and moral decision to which he feels them challenging and summoning him. Under the impression of these writings his attitude toward the world and toward man begins to change. His naive confidence that the cultivation of the mind and its steady progress would suffice to make man better, freer and happier is shaken. He feels he must apply leverage at a different point if the question of the "vocation of man" is to be made susceptible of philosophic solution. All the judgments Kant ventures on Rousseau's character and disposition point in the same direction. He feels the paradox

[6] *Fragments,* 618.

of this disposition. It does not, however, repel him, but
rather attracts him, because he thinks he discerns in Rousseau the will not to be peculiar and eccentric but to be altogether sincere. He does not yield to the suspicion that all
Rousseau's paradoxical theses are merely artificial, that he
is using his "extraordinary talents and magic power of eloquence" only in order to "affect an eccentricity that would
surpass all intellectual rivals by its captivating and aston-
ishing novelty."[7] He tries to penetrate to the ultimate
foundation of Rousseau's position, and he finds it not only
in a special mode of thought but in a certain "mood" of
the spirit to which he feels attracted and which strikes in
him a responsive chord.

In what respect could two such different and opposite
natures meet, and on what ideals could they agree? If we
raise this question, we discover to our surprise that Kant
understood and prized just those things in Rousseau that
were inaccessible to the group among whom Rousseau
lived. If we follow the account in Rousseau's *Confessions*
and supplement it with what we know from his correspondence, we recognize the reason for the tragic misunderstanding which ruined his life. Certainly Rousseau's disposition,
his sensitiveness, his violence, his morbid distrust, contributed to this misunderstanding. But these traits were
by no means the only reason for it. What even Rousseau's
closest friends could not understand or forgive him was the
solitude in which he took refuge. At first they saw in this
desire for solitude only a fleeting impulse that would soon
pass, and they interpreted his persistent resolution as an
incomprehensible stubbornness.

This trait was responsible for the break with Diderot.
All Diderot's letters express a genuinely friendly interest
and a real sympathy for Rousseau's fate. But all Diderot's

[7] *Fragments*, 624.

keenness of insight deserts him, otherwise so penetrating a psychologist, when confronted by Rousseau's personality. As is well known, Rousseau felt wounded to the extreme when in Diderot's *Fils Naturel* he read that "only the evil man seeks solitude." He never forgave Diderot these words. We may well believe Diderot's repeated assurance that the statement was not aimed at Rousseau. But on the other hand there existed here a genuine opposition of spirit which was bound to make itself more and more clearly felt as time went by and which in the end proved irreconcilable.

Diderot's whole thought moves within and is bound up with a specific social order. The *Encyclopedia* he edited took as its essential task to raise thought to a social level, to make it a function not of the individual but of society. Whatever Diderot accomplished was possible for him only because he was full of this enterprise and devoted all his powers of understanding and will to its service. And as he himself thought with and for Parisian society, he stood constantly in need of that society to stimulate his thinking and keep it active. His work could prosper only in the atmosphere of the Paris salons. Despite all his enthusiasm for nature, to which he too was devoted, he could not free himself from this standard, and he set up the same standard for Rousseau as well, with a naïveté that strikes us today as strange.

To Diderot, Rousseau's life in the "Hermitage" seemed an expression of morbid over-stimulation, and he can hardly speak of it save with bitterness and irony. Even in the letters he wrote Rousseau to effect a reconciliation and to allay his distrust, this bitterness appears. To one he even adds a contemptuous postscript: "Farewell, citizen," he writes, "what an extraordinary citizen a hermit is."[8]

[8] Letter from Diderot, March 10, 1757 (*C.G.*, III, No. 342, p. 20).

(C'est pourtant un citoyen bien singulier qu'un Hermite.) But in fact and in all seriousness Rousseau was just such a *citoyen bien singulier.* From the outset he stood in a paradoxical relation to society: he had to flee from it in order to serve it and to give it what he was capable of giving. In his hermitage he reflected upon the duties of citizenship, and only there did he become the author of the *Social Contract.* In the *Émile* also he retained the same trait: he requires that Émile be educated *outside* society, because in this way alone can he be educated *for* society in the only true sense.

All this Kant discerned. He gave himself up to the direct impression received from studying the *Émile,* and he thus gained a deeper insight into Rousseau's nature than the people among whom Rousseau lived and even his closest friends were capable of. For he was not blinded by prejudices. He neither exaggerated the value of life in society nor underestimated it. Kant was by no means unsociable; he sought and cherished social intercourse and saw in it an intellectual and moral discipline. Especially in his youth he yielded himself freely to the charm of such relations; "Magister" Kant was much sought after in all circles of Königsberg society, among merchants and army officers, by the middle class as well as the nobility; he was accounted an excellent conversationalist and man of the world. But if Kant possessed such advantages and if he sought to cultivate and perfect them, they were never capable of deluding him. He saw in them a grace and ornament of life, but nothing capable of constituting and determining its real worth. For him the demands of "mores" and of "morality" were quite distinct. And he was grateful to Rousseau because in an age when the best minds seemed to have forgotten this distinction, he drew the line with utter and thoroughgoing precision.

Kant regarded this as Rousseau's distinctive achievement. He did not think that Rousseau intended to alienate men from civilization or to lead them back to the wilderness by his enthusiastic praise of the state of nature. He explicitly defends him from such a suspicion, to which Voltaire had given so sharp and biting an expression. In his lectures on anthropology he declared that "it is surely not permissible to regard Rousseau's splenetic account of the human race that has dared to desert the state of nature, as a commendation of returning to this condition in the forests. His writings . . . did not indeed propose that man should *go* back to the state of nature, but that he should *look* back upon it from the level he has now attained."[9]

From this remark of Kant's it is quite clear in what sense he took Rousseau's doctrine of the "state of nature," and in what direction he developed it further. In it he saw —to express it in terms of his own subsequent ideas—not a constitutive but a regulative principle. He regarded Rousseau's theory not as a theory of what exists but of what should be, not as an account of what has been but as an expression of what ought to be, not as a retrospective elegy but as a prospective prophecy. For Kant the seemingly retrospective view should serve to equip men for the future and to make them fit to establish that future. It should not alienate men from the task of improving their civilization, but should show them how much in the values they prize in civilization is sham and show. This distinction is fundamental for Kant also; for him every genuine ordering of the values in human life and experience depends upon it. For him none of the merely social "virtues," no matter how glamorous they may seem, could ever constitute the true meaning of "virtue" itself. "Every social virtue of man

[9] *Anthropology*, par. 107 (*Werke*, VIII, 221).

is but a token," his anthropology declares; "he who takes it for real gold is but a child." [10]

For Kant all the goods of civilization have their "value," but this value does not suffice to assure them of genuine "worth." For Kant's ethics draws a sharp dividing line between the two. "In the realm of ends," declares the *Fundamentals of the Metaphysics of Morals*, "everything has either a value or a worth. What has a value has a substitute which can replace it as its equivalent; but whatever is, on the other hand, exalted above all values, and thus lacks an equivalent, . . . has no merely relative value, that is, a price, but rather an inner worth, that is, dignity. Now morality is the condition in accordance with which alone a reasonable being can be an end in himself, because only through morality is it possible to be an autonomous member of the realm of ends. Hence morality, and humanity, in so far as it is capable of morality, can alone possess dignity." [11]

For the moment let us not pursue the significance these words possess for Kant's theory of freedom and for the construction of his system. We shall ask merely how Rousseau's figure must have appeared to him in the light of this conviction. And here we can at once establish a characteristic difference as over against the judgment of most of his contemporaries. Kant was perhaps the first to do justice to that trait in Rousseau's nature which even his closest friends misunderstood. Rousseau gave repeated assurances in his writings, in his *Confessions* and in his letters, that he never loved men more warmly than when he seemed to be drawing away and fleeing from them. In contact with people and under the compulsion of social conventions, Rousseau could not discover the human nature he was

[10] *Anthropology*, par. 14 (*Werke*, VIII, 38).
[11] *Werke*, IV, 293.

capable of loving. "I was never made for society," he writes at the end of his life in the *Rêveries du promeneur solitaire*, "where everything is compulsion and burdensome obligation. My independent disposition always made it impossible for me to bow to all that those who wish to live among men must accept. As soon as I can act freely I am good and do only what is good; but as soon as I feel the yoke of men I become rebellious and headstrong—and then I am nothing."[12]

This form of "misanthropy," derived from the desire to protect his independence under all circumstances, Kant understood—and approved. He gave a very attractive and characteristic account of the type of personality that corresponds to it in the sketch of the "melancholy temperament" incorporated in his *Observations on the Feeling of the Beautiful and the Sublime.* There is little doubt that Rousseau contributed essential features to this portrait of "the melancholy man." "The man of melancholy disposition is little concerned with the judgment of others, with their opinion of what is good or true; he relies purely on his own insight. Because his motivating forces assume the nature of fundamental principles, he cannot readily be turned to other thoughts; his perseverance can at times degenerate into obstinacy. He regards changes of fashion with indifference and their glitter with contempt. . . . He has a lofty sense of the dignity of human nature. He esteems himself and regards man as a creature deserving of respect. He suffers no abject subservience and breathes the noble air of freedom. To him all chains are abhorrent, from the gilded fetters worn at court to the heavy irons of the galley slave. He is a stern judge of himself as well as of others and is not infrequently disgusted with himself as well as with the world."[13]

[12] *Rêveries,* VI, 280.   [13] *Werke,* II, 261.

All this is not merely characteristic of Kant's individual ideas; it provides more than a purely biographical interest. It offers an important clue in the history of ideas, for it reveals an aspect of Rousseau's influence unjustifiably neglected in the traditional view we are accustomed to hold of his effect on modern intellectual history. This traditional view was molded historically by the "Age of Genius" and by Romanticism. In Germany it was the generation of "Storm and Stress" that saw in Rousseau their ancestor and patron. This generation regarded him as the prophet of a new gospel of nature and as the thinker who had rediscovered the primitive power of the emotions and passions and had emancipated them from all restrictions, from the restriction of convention as well as that of "reason." Modern criticism also has not infrequently accepted this conception, and based on it all the charges it has brought against Rousseau, the visionary, dreamer and enthusiast.

But during the sixties of the eighteenth century, in the crucial period for Rousseau's influence on Kant, men saw his teaching in another light. For this period Rousseau was not in the first instance the restorer of the rights of the emotions, the apostle of "sentimentality"; he was, as Kant calls him, "the restorer of the rights of humanity." Not only Kant but Lessing also passed such a judgment. Lessing, the most circumspect and manly mind of the age, was surely not disposed to let himself be overcome by frenzy of emotion or to argue the case for sentimentality in any form. Yet Rousseau's work did not fail to have its influence on him also. In his notice of Rousseau's first *Discourse* he praised the "elevated attitudes" of the essay and the "manly eloquence" with which they were presented. And he declared that we must feel a secret respect for a man who dared "to speak for virtue against all accepted prejudices," even if he went too far in his conclusions.[14]

Kant thought and felt exactly the same way. He too did not pass over the *New Héloise* without sympathy. "In the very same spirit in which he examined Leibniz, Wolff, Baumgarten, Crusius and Hume," Herder reports of Kant during the 'sixties, "he took up the writings of Rousseau, then just appearing, his Émile and his Héloise . . . appraised them and returned again and again to an unaffected insight into nature and the moral worth of man."[15] But Kant certainly read the *New Héloise* in different fashion from most of his contemporaries and from most readers of later times. For him the center of gravity of the whole lay not in the romantic love story but in the second, "moral" portion of the work. He did not regard this as a mere unrelated supplement with which Rousseau had disfigured his work and weakened his artistic effect; and so he could not look upon the *New Héloise* as a mere sentimental romance or a glorification of passion. "Rousseau's state of nature," according to Irving Babbitt, "is only the projection of his own temperament and its dominant desires upon the void. His programme amounts in practice to the indulgence of infinite indeterminate desire, to an endless and aimless vagabondage of the emotions with the imagination as their free accomplice."[16]

Had this really been Rousseau's "program," Kant could not have felt attracted to it at any time of his life and thought; he would have turned from it with indignation. But even in the *New Héloise* he found something quite different by keeping in mind the total character of the work. "I trusted my nature, and followed my impulses,"

[14] Lessing's notice of Rousseau's first *Discourse*, April, 1751. Cf. *Werke*, Lachmann-Muncker ed., IV, 387ff.

[15] Herder, *Briefe zur Beförderung der Humanität*, 79th letter (*Werke*, Suphan ed., XVII, 404).

[16] Babbitt, *Rousseau and Romanticism* (Boston, 1919), 79.

he read in Julie's letters. "A happy instinct leads me to the good; a violent passion arises; it has its source in that same instinct: what shall I do to destroy it? From the consideration of order I derive beauty and virtue . . . but what can they do against my private interest? . . . Finally, since the character and the love of the beautiful are imprinted by nature in the depths of my soul, I shall have my rule as long as they are not disfigured. But how can I be sure that I shall always preserve in its purity that inner image which finds among sensible things no model with which it may be compared? Do we not know that the disordered affections corrupt the judgment as they corrupt the will? . . . For the heart deceives us in a thousand ways and acts only by a principle always suspect, but reason has no other end than what is good, its rules are certain, clear and easy in conduct, and it never goes astray save in the useless speculations that are not made for it."[17]

In such words limiting and opposing the doctrine of the "omnipotence of the heart" Kant, unlike many modern critics, did not see mere sophistical disguises of Rousseau's ideas; he thought rather that he here found their true and essential meaning. Thus he felt strengthened by Rousseau himself to distrust the ideal of the "beautiful soul" (*schöne Seele*) emphasized by eighteenth century ethics. He did not reject this ideal, but declared that from it there could be derived no principle for the scientific and philosophic foundation of ethics. Such a principle he sought not in the beauty of feeling but in the sublimity of the will. "Among moral qualities only true virtue is sublime. There are to be sure good moral qualities that are amiable and fine and that, in so far as they are in harmony with virtue, can also be regarded as noble, although they cannot

[17] *Nouvelle Héloise,* Pt. III, letters 18 and 20 (Mornet ed., III, 66f., 85).

be reckoned as belonging to a virtuous disposition. In such matters judgment is nice and complicated. . . . A certain tender-heartedness that springs from a warm feeling of sympathy is fine and amiable, for it indicates a kindly interest in the fate of other men. . . . But this good-natured passion is weak and always blind. . . . When on the other hand universal good-will has become a principle for you, to which you always subordinate your actions, then love for the suffering still remains, but it has now been transformed from a higher standpoint into the true relation to your whole duty. . . . As soon as this feeling has attained its proper universality, it is sublime, but at the same time colder. For it is not possible to fill our hearts with tender sympathy for every man and to be bathed in sorrow at the distress of every stranger, or else the virtuous man, forever dissolved in tears of sympathy, would get no farther with all this good-nature than a tender-hearted idler."[18]

This was written in 1764, in the *Observations on the Feeling of the Beautiful and the Sublime*—but it already contains the characteristic attitude of Kant's later ethics. It is obvious that with this attitude and conviction Kant could not stop with Rousseau, that he must feel much in him to be strange and fantastic. For high as his moral ideals could aspire, Rousseau himself was never safe from relapses into another way of feeling. He has described in his *Confessions* how in his love for Mme. d'Houdetot he was transformed from the philosopher, the critic of society, the apostle of freedom, into the "extravagant shepherd" again. "See the grave citizen of Geneva," he cried out in pain, "see the austere Jean-Jacques, almost forty-five, become all at once again the extravagant shepherd."[19] But Kant, usually so strict, was not misled by

[18] *Werke*, II, 255f.   [19] *Confessions*, Bk. IX, 332.

such "extravagances" in his admiration for Rousseau's writings and in his reverence for his person. He expressly defends Rousseau against the charge of being a mere visionary. "I place Aristides among usurers, Epictetus among courtiers, and Jean-Jacques Rousseau among the doctors of the Sorbonne. I think I hear a loud mocking laughter, and a hundred voices crying, '*What visionaries!*' This ambiguous appearance of being a blind idealist in moral feelings that are in themselves good is *enthusiasm,* and never has anything great been accomplished in the world without it."[20] Thus Kant made clear in the example of Rousseau the truth of Plato's words about the Θεία μανία.

What always reconciled Kant again to Rousseau, with all his paradoxical and enthusiastic qualities, was the fearlessness, the independence of thought and feeling, the will to the "unconditioned" he there encountered. For Kant himself, though far from any rebellion against the constituted authorities, was inspired with the strongest sense of independence. Much that surprises us in his way of life and may at times seem strange or eccentric, is explained by this trait of his character: by the desire to preserve his inner and outer independence in every moment of life and under all circumstances. And his ethical theory also reckons independence among the highest moral goods. "In submissiveness there is not only something exceedingly dangerous," he says in his notes to the *Observations on the Feeling of the Beautiful and the Sublime,* "but also a certain ugliness and a contradiction, which at the same time indicates its illegitimacy. An animal is not yet a complete being, because it is not conscious of itself . . . it knows nothing of its own existence. But that man himself should stand in need of no soul and have no will of his

[20] *Werke,* II, 311.

own, and that another soul should move his limbs, this is absurd and perverse. Such a man is like the mere tool of another. . . . The man who stands in dependence on another is no longer a man, he has lost his standing, he is nothing but the possession of another man."[21] In this conviction Kant approached Rousseau, and in it he could greet him as a philosophical liberator.

II. ROUSSEAU AND THE DOCTRINE OF HUMAN NATURE

KANT could accord Rousseau's thought no higher praise than to place it side by side with Newton's work: "Newton was the first to discern order and regularity in combination with great simplicity, where before him men had encountered disorder and unrelated diversity. Since Newton the comets follow geometric orbits. Rousseau was the first to discover beneath the varying forms human nature assumes, the deeply concealed essence of man and the hidden law in accordance with which Providence is justified by his observations. Before them, the objections of King Alfonso and the Manichaeans were still valid. After Newton and Rousseau, the ways of God are justified—and Pope's thesis is henceforth true."[22]

At first glance there can hardly be a stranger parallel than Kant is here attempting. For where is the actual basis of comparison? Rousseau never posed as an empirical investigator claiming to have reduced man's life and being to general laws that could be known and formulated with

---

[21] *Fragments*, VIII, 635f.

[22] *Fragments*, VIII, 630. King Alfonso of Castile, according to the anecdote, after having studied the Ptolemaic system of astronomy, is supposed to have found the system of the universe very irregular and confusing. "If I had been the Creator of the world," he said, "I should have made the thing better."

precision. The eighteenth century held to its faith in reason and science and saw in them "des Menschen allerhöchste Kraft," man's supreme power. It was convinced that it would take only the complete development of man's understanding, only the cultivation of all his intellectual powers, to transform man spiritually and to produce a new and happier humanity. But Rousseau had broken with this faith; to it he had opposed that passionate indictment against the arts and sciences contained in his first *Discourse*. How could Kant, whose real genius lay in his ability to make clear and precise distinctions, think of comparing two such different achievements as those of Newton and Rousseau? How could he elevate Rousseau's notion of the "state of nature" to the level of a scientific discovery?

Rousseau's own account of the genesis of the *Discourse on Inequality* is convincing evidence that he himself had a rather different intention and purpose in mind. He did not arrive at the picture he here draws of man's original state through any abstract conceptual analysis; it came to him almost like a vision. He tells how the initial plan of his work occurred to him on long walks in the woods about Saint-Germain. "Deep in the heart of the forest I sought and found the vision of those primeval ages whose history I bravely sketched. I denied myself all the easy deceits to which men are prone. I dared to unveil human nature and to look upon it in its nakedness, to trace the course of times and of events which have disfigured human nature. And while comparing conventional man (*l'homme de l'homme*) with natural man, I pointed out the true source of our misery in our pretended perfection." [23]

Why, then, did Kant see in all this anything but an idle dream, he who was so hostile to all visionary tendencies and who mocked the metaphysicians of his day as "airy

[23] *Confessions*, VIII, 269.

architects of intellectual worlds" when they attempted to go beyond experience and to transcend it on principle? What value could the Rousseauian distinction between an *homme de la nature* and an *homme de l'homme* possess for him? In this distinction he saw neither an historical description of mankind's course of development nor an evolutionary hypothesis. He saw in it rather a contribution to ethical and social criticism, a discrimination of true and false values. And he welcomed this discrimination.

· What Kant prized in Rousseau was the fact that he had distinguished more clearly than others between the mask that man wears and his actual visage. For Kant, too, there are innumerable apparent "goods" in civilization which add nothing to man's moral worth and in fact even obscure it and render it problematic. There is a great deal that man has absorbed in the course of time and learned from his cultural heritage, which is really in conflict with his "true" character and his proper and original vocation. Thus Kant never takes the idea of the *homme naturel* in a purely scientific or historical sense, but rather ethically and teleologically. What is truly permanent in human nature is not any condition *in which* it once existed and *from which* it has fallen; rather it is the goal *for which* and toward which it moves. Kant looks for constancy not in what man *is* but in what he *should be*. And Kant credits Rousseau the ethical philosopher with having discerned the "real man" beneath all the distortions and concealments, beneath all the masks that man has created for himself and worn in the course of his history. That is, Kant esteems Rousseau for having recognized and honored man's distinctive and unchanging end. His aim was to advance further along this path Rousseau had taken, and he sought to go on to the goal.

We know that this was the enterprise he made central

in his academic teaching during the 'sixties. "Since in Ethics I always undertake an historical and philosophic consideration of what occurs before I point out what should occur," Kant states in announcing his lectures for the year 1765-66, "I shall set forth the method by which we must study man—man not only in the varying forms in which his accidental circumstances have molded him, in the distorted form in which even philosophers have almost always misconstrued him, but what is enduring in human nature, and the proper place of man in creation."[24] According to Kant it is precisely the empirical philosophers, those who derive their doctrine from experience and aim to base a knowledge of human nature on the history of man's previous development, who have failed to face this task. They have seen only the changing and accidental, not the essential and permanent. Rousseau sharpened Kant's awareness of this "essential" element which, he held, consists of man's ethical and not his physical nature. On this account he salutes Rousseau's point of view as a new epoch in the thinking of mankind, "a great discovery of our age" totally unknown to the ancients.[25]

To be sure, a thinker like Kant had available an intellectual equipment for the achievement of his purpose entirely different from Rousseau's. As a follower of Newton he did not, indeed, aim to found metaphysics on experience, but to limit it to the realm of possible experience. He insisted that at all points it establish itself upon observed phenomena, and that it carry out a strict analysis of these phenomena. "We are still far from the time," declares Kant in 1763 in his *Enquiry into the Evidences of the Principles of Natural Theology and Morals,* "when we can proceed synthetically in metaphysics; only when analysis has helped us to attain clear and explicitly understood concepts will

[24] *Werke,* II, 326.   [25] *ibid.*

synthesis be able to derive complicated cognitions from the simplest, as in mathematics."[26]

Because of this basic methodological conviction Kant must refuse to follow Rousseau wherever the latter proceeds in purely deductive fashion, where he treats the assumed "state of nature" as an established fact from which to draw conclusions. Metaphysics must not be based upon invented or hypothetically improvised facts; it must begin with what is given, with empirically ascertained data. And in this sense our only datum is civilized man, not the Rousseauian savage who wanders alone in the forests. Thus even if he does not disallow the value of the problem which Rousseau set up, Kant must here reverse his method of procedure. "Rousseau," he declares, "proceeds synthetically and begins with natural man; I proceed analytically and begin with civilized man."[27] This beginning is indicated because in the concept of man civilization constitutes no secondary or accidental characteristic but marks man's essential nature, his specific character. He who would study animals must start with them in their wild state; but he who would know man must observe him in his creative power and his creative achievement, that is, in his civilization.[28]

But if the student of ethics must accept and build on the "fact of civilization" in this sense—just as, in his theory of knowledge, Kant had begun with the "fact" of mathematics and mathematical natural science—this does not imply that he must exempt this fundamental fact from critical consideration. Here too he must distinguish between the accidental and the necessary, and in this distinction Kant discerns the most important task of philosophy.

[26] *Werke*, II, 191.   [27] *Fragments*, VIII, 613.
[28] *Reflexionen Kants zur kritischen Philosophie*. Ed. by Benno Erdmann (Leipzig, 1882), No. 648; I, 205.

"If there is any science man really needs," he declares, with a high sense of the mission of the critical philosophy, "it is the one I teach, of how to occupy properly that place in creation that is assigned to man, and how to learn from it what one must be in order to be a man. Granted that he may have become acquainted with deceptive allurements above him or below him, which have unconsciously enticed him away from his distinctive station, then this teaching will lead him back again to the human level, and however small or deficient he may regard himself, he will suit his assigned station, because he will be just what he should be." [29]

For Kant man's "assigned station" is not located in nature alone; for he must raise himself above it, above all merely vegetative or animal life. But it is just as far from lying somewhere outside nature, in something absolutely other-worldly or transcendent. Man should seek the real law of his being and his conduct neither below nor above himself; he should derive it from himself, and should fashion himself in accordance with the determination of his own free will. For this he requires life in society as well as an inner freedom from social standards and an independent judgment of conventional social values. Even after completing his critical system, Kant declared in his *Idea of a Universal History in the Interest of World Citizenship* (1784), "Rousseau was not so mistaken in giving preference to the condition of the savage, if we omit the last step our species still has to mount. We are cultivated to a high degree by art and science. We are civilized to excess by all sorts of social niceties and refinements. But to consider ourselves truly ethical much is still lacking. . . . So long as . . . states use all their power for vain and violent expansion and thus constantly obstruct the slow

[29] *Fragments*, VIII, 624f.

efforts of their citizens towards inner development . . . we can expect nothing of this sort, because such a development demands a lengthy inner reworking of every commonwealth to foster the education of its citizens. But all good not based on morally good intention is nothing but vain illusion and splendid misery."[30]

In thus extending Rousseau's central idea, Kant freed it from an ambiguity which has always made it hard to understand, and still does today. In Rousseau himself it is never entirely clear to what extent his notion of a state of nature is "ideal" and to what extent it is "empirical." He is always shifting from a factual to a purely ideal interpretation. In the preface to his *Discourse on the Origin and Foundation of Inequality* he expressly emphasizes the latter: he declares that he is starting from a state of human affairs that no longer exists, that perhaps never existed and will probably never exist, but which we must nevertheless posit in order to judge rightly our present state. But Rousseau did not always speak this way. Often enough he confused his role as educator, as social critic and moral philosopher with the role of the historian. "O man, whatever country thou belongest to," he exclaims, "whatever be thy opinions, hearken: behold thy history, as I have tried to read it, not in the books of thy fellows who are liars, but in nature, which never lies."[31] And in the final review Rousseau gave of his whole work in his *Rousseau Judge of Jean-Jacques,* he maintained this interpretation: he here describes himself as the first truthful "historian of human nature."

Such a value Kant never attributed to Rousseau's ideas; from the start he was too acute a critic not to see the contrast existing between ethical truths based on reason and

[30] *Werke*, IV, 161.
[31] *Discourse on Inequality* (Vaughan, I, 142).

historical truths based on facts. Hence he applied to Rousseau's work what he called the "art of reflective analysis," which in the *Critique of Practical Reason* he himself compares with the analysis of the chemist. The man who introduced anthropology as a branch of study in German universities and who lectured on it regularly for decades was too well-grounded an empiricist in this realm to follow Rousseau's lead. Kant framed no hypotheses concerning the original state of mankind. If he once ventured a step in this direction, in the essay on the *Conjectural Beginning of Human History* (1786), he declared emphatically that he was proposing no strict scientific theory but a "mere excursion" of the imagination accompanied by reason.[32] In Rousseau's own theses, however, Kant made a sharp distinction between the "historical" and the "rational"— and even in accepting the latter he regarded it not in terms of theoretical but of "practical reason," and judged it by the latter's standards. Rousseau was always for him the thinker who, in the realm of ethics, "awakened him from dogmatic slumber"—who had confronted him with new questions and stimulated him to new solutions.

III. LAW AND THE STATE

KANT judged that Rousseau's purpose did not involve inviting man to go back to the state of nature, but rather to look back to it in order to become aware of the errors and weaknesses of conventional society. This interpretation finds its best confirmation in Rousseau's ideas on law and the state. Those critics of Rousseau who see in him nothing but the Romantic enthusiast have never done justice to this part of his thought. They have felt it an incomprehensible inconsistency and an abandonment of his own central posi-

[32] *Werke*, IV, 327.

tion that the very Rousseau who in the *Discourse on the Origin and Foundation of Inequality* had declared war on society and made it responsible for all the ills of mankind, should now, in the *Social Contract,* aim to write the laws for that society—laws which should indeed bind the individual to the group with duties far stricter and stronger than ever before.

But Rousseau expressly protested against such objections, which he did not escape even during his lifetime, in that self-examination of his life and work which he undertook at the end of his career in his *Rousseau Judge of Jean-Jacques.* He explains that it had never been his intention, even in his earliest writings, to try to turn back the wheel of history and to restore man once more to that starting-point from which he had set forth. "Human nature does not go back": man cannot at will reverse the direction he has once taken—he cannot go back, only ahead. The wounds the existing structure of society has inflicted on mankind cannot be healed by destroying the instrument that caused them. We must look further; we must attack not the instrument but the hand that guided it. It is not the form of the social contract as such that is at fault; it is rather the will that inspires the contract. So long as that will is bound to the service of individuals or groups that have gained special privilege through power or wealth, it is the source of all the evil, the champion and protector of all the suffering and injustice that men can inflict on one another.

But this is by no means the natural function of the social will; it is rather its corruption. The state too has a "nature" of its own to which Rousseau wants to restore it, even though this nature consists not in an initial condition but in a primary function. This function is the administration of law and the establishment of justice. In his theory of the state Rousseau was from the outset a Platonist: Plato's *Republic* early became one of his favorite texts. If as a eudemonist he sought passionately to bring about human happiness, he was obliged to recognize more and more clearly that the effort was vain so long as the "rights of man" were insecure. As secretary of the embassy in Venice, Rousseau acquired an insight into the way in which political and diplomatic affairs were transacted under the reigning regime, which served to strengthen and deepen this conviction. And now, in this most essential and difficult task, he did not allow himself to be swept away, as in his first writings, by an excess of enthusiasm and emotion. He carried the draft of his *Political Institutions* about with him for thirteen or fourteen years; he did not mention it even to his closest friends like Diderot. He felt the difficulty of the task weighing on him, and was conscious of his responsibility. "I had attained the insight," he declares in his *Confessions,* "that everything is at bottom dependent on political arrangements, and that no matter what position one takes, a people will never be otherwise than what its form of government makes it."[38] The lever must be placed at this point. The dream of human happiness evaporates if we do not succeed in helping the Rights of Man to attain victory.

When Rousseau examines the available forms of a "political philosophy," he finds them all insufficient and without foundation. According to him Plato alone discerned the real problem, while all his successors misconstrued or at least warped it. The Aristotelian doctrine that man is "by nature" a social being, a ζῷον πολιτικόν, Rousseau rejects. He does not believe in that "social instinct" on which the theorists of the seventeenth and eighteenth centuries hoped to found society. In this respect he

[38] *Confessions,* IX, 296.

disputes the theory of Grotius as well as that of Diderot and the Encyclopedists. It is not man's physical nature or any sort of originally implanted need which drives him to his fellows. By nature man has but a single instinct—the instinct of self-preservation. This basic demand *suum esse conservare* man must renounce as soon as he enters society. He has now lost his *indépendance naturelle*, and the lost paradise of this independence can never be restored once he has taken the first step outside. Never again can he find "himself"; he is entangled in a thousand claims and demands addressed to him from without. Hence the man who has a true sense of independence, the *homme indépendant* Rousseau describes in his earliest political sketches, will never willingly bow beneath the yoke of society. He will soon discover the basic defect, the sophism in principle, in all the "legal grounds" that philosophic theory has invented as the foundation of society.[34]

But if we must abandon the idea of an original social instinct uniting men, then the only theory of the state that seems to be left is that of which among the moderns Hobbes is the keenest and most important representative. Instead of seeing society as the result of an instinct of "sympathy," we must regard it as a product of the sheer instinct for power. It is based on power, and only by power can it be preserved. Rousseau went indeed so far in his attack on Grotius and the Encyclopedists as to hail Hobbes as his ally against them. For a time he saw in Hobbes the great political realist, and as such he preferred Hobbes to all those who have painted human society in charming colors. In one of his essays he called Hobbes one of the

---

[34] This point of view is expressed with particular clarity in the first draft of the *Social Contract* which Vaughan has published. Cf. *The Political Writings of Rousseau*, ed. C. E. Vaughan, 2 vols. (Cambridge, 1915), I, 449ff.

greatest philosophers and one of the most eminent men of genius.[35] "If a universal society existed anywhere save in the systems of philosophers," he argues, "it would be a moral entity with distinctive characteristics that could be differentiated from those of the individual constituents out of which it was constructed. There would be a universal language that nature would teach to all men and that would constitute the most important instrument for their mutual intercourse. There would be a kind of common organ of sensation (*sensorium commune*) that would perceive events wherever they occurred. The public weal or woe would not only be composed, as in a simple aggregate, of the happiness or unhappiness of individuals; it would consist of that tie that binds them all to one another."[36]

But such a "universal tie," such a "general will," cannot be demonstrated as an empirical fact, and therefore according to Rousseau the empiricist Hobbes was right in denying it. But he vigorously disputes all the consequences that Hobbes as a moralist deduced from this denial. In Hobbes's theory of the power state, Rousseau, the reader and admirer of Plato, recognized the position that Thrasymachus develops in the first book of the *Republic*. And by virtue of this agreement he finds in Hobbes's ideas a mere rebirth of the views of the Sophists, which provide no foundation for law but annihilate it.[37]

What, then, remains after the idyll of an original social impulse in human nature has been destroyed, and after Hobbes's account of the "war of all against all" is recognized as a paradoxical exaggeration and caricature? On what foundation can we still erect society if we regard both types of hypothesis as mere creatures of speculation?

---

[35] Vaughan, I, 305.
[36] *Social Contract,* first draft, Vaughan, I, 449f.
[37] Cf. *Political Writings,* ed. Vaughan, I, 306.

What is the true nature of the "social bond," which no political theory has as yet really revealed? From Rousseau's first draft of the *Social Contract* we can see that for him this was the question out of which grew the conception of his work.[88] And the answer he gives opens up new and original lines of thought.

It is one of the most remarkable features of Rousseau's ideas, and one most frequently misunderstood, that he who was the true champion of feeling and of the "rights of the heart" most emphatically denied the primacy of feeling in his theory of law and of the state. He must seek a different foundation for legal and political institutions, for in his view they are constructs of the will and are therefore subject to a law of their own, a mode of law *sui generis*. It is in the nature of the state that it should not aim at fusing feelings into a unity, but rather at unifying acts of the will and directing them to a common goal. It fulfills this function only if it really succeeds in such a unification, that is, if every demand it makes on the individual is regarded and accepted by him as an expression of the common will. Hence for Rousseau the real "social bond" consists in the fact that particular individuals and groups are not called upon to rule over others; for such a rule, in no matter what refined or "civilized" forms it were exercised, could only reduce us to the most abject slavery. This slavery disappears only if law as such assumes guidance and leadership, and if in their mutual relations one man does not obey another, but a common subordination to law takes the place of such service and obedience.

This enthusiasm for law as the "universal voice" fills all Rousseau's political writings and sketches. In his article on *Political Economy* he asks: "How can it happen that

[88] First draft of the *Social Contract,* chap. v: *Fausses notions du lien social,* Vaughan, I, 462ff.

[30]

men obey without having anyone above them to issue commands, that they serve without having a master, that they are all the freer when each of them, acting under an apparent compulsion, loses only that part of his freedom with which he can injure others? These wonders are the work of Law. It is to Law alone that men owe justice and liberty; it is this salutary organ of the will of all that makes obligatory the natural equality between men; it is this heavenly voice that dictates to each citizen the precepts of public reason, and teaches him to act in accordance with the maxims of his own judgment, and not to be in contradiction to himself."[39]

At this point, according to Rousseau, we first find the true conception of the "social bond" (*lien social*). For such a bond must bind together freely acting persons, not dead things. Hence it cannot be something imposed upon the wills of these persons from without; they must constitute and create it themselves. Accordingly all theories fail which seek to derive the "social contract" in any form from a contract involving subjection, from a *pactum subjectionis*. With Hobbes we may take as the origin of such a contract of subjection, an agreement between rulers and ruled; with Grotius we may base it on an actual enslavement in the course of conquest—but in any case the chief objection remains the same. For in this way only a union *de facto* could have come about, never one *de jure*. "There will always be a great difference," Rousseau declares, "between subduing a multitude and ruling a society. Even if scattered individuals were successively enslaved by one man, no matter how numerous they might be, I still see nothing more than a master and his slaves, certainly not a people and its ruler; I see what may be

<hr>

[39] "Political Economy," Vaughan, I, 245.

termed an aggregation but not an association; there is as yet neither public good nor body politic."[40]

We need no detailed demonstration to show how the attitude expressed in these phrases must have affected Kant. We hear their echo and reverberations in the most essential and crucial theses of the Kantian ethics. The "fundamental law of pure practical reason": "Act so that the maxim of thy will can always at the same time hold good as a principle of universal legislation," coincides with what Rousseau regards as the really fundamental principle of every "legitimate" social order. And we may surmise that Rousseau not only influenced the content and systematic development of Kant's foundation of ethics, but that he also formed its language and style.

This is particularly evident in the second striking formulation of the "categorical imperative," which Kant proposed in his *Fundamental Principles of the Metaphysics of Morals:* "So act as to treat humanity, whether in thine own person or in that of any other, in every case as an end withal, never as means merely."[41] If in the first expression of the categorical imperative, which places the emphasis on "universal legislation," we recognize Rousseau the political theorist, the philosopher of the *volonté générale,* the second formulation takes us back to the main ideas of Rousseau's theory of education. Central to his educational theory is the requirement that the pupil is to be educated for his own sake, not for others. He should be developed to manhood, but to "natural" not to "artificial" manhood, to be *homme naturel* not *homme artificiel.* And for this reason we must not approach him at an early age with demands that have their source only in the utterly artificial and conventional structure of contemporary society. Instead of forcing him

[40] *Social Contract,* I, v (Vaughan, II, 31).
[41] *Werke,* IV, 287.

into the straitjacket of these conventions, we should awaken in him a sense of independence; instead of making him serve the purposes of others, we should teach him to think of himself as an end and to act in accordance with this idea. Only when he has become in this sense inwardly free is he to enter society, and only then will he be able to contribute to it in the right way; for only the free man is the true citizen. This is the underlying theme of the *Émile*, and this is the maxim that Rousseau has Mme. de Wolmar express in the later sections of the *New Héloise*: "Man is too noble a being to serve simply as the instrument for others, and he must not be used for what suits them without consulting also what suits himself. . . . It is never right to harm a human soul for the advantage of others."[42]

But here too, however closely Kant approached the content of Rousseau's thought, he made a significant change in its methodological foundation, and thus he first freed it from various ambiguities that were present in Rousseau's own presentation. The complaint has at times been made with justice that Rousseau called his chief political work the *Social Contract* instead of retaining the "neutral" title *De la société civile* he had previously intended.[43] For the designation "social contract" is bound up by an age-old tradition of natural law with all sorts of secondary associations that have no connection with the actual task Rousseau set himself. It suggests the idea of a temporal beginning of society, of a single act by which it was once brought into being. Rousseau, to be sure, insisted that for him it was not a question of any such beginning, but of the "princi-

[42] *Nouvelle Héloise,* v, letter 2; IV, 22.
[43] Cf. Vaughan, Preface to his edition of the *Political Writings,* I, 22.

ple" of society, that he was concerned with a problem of legal philosophy, not of history.

In this respect he drew a sharp line between his own problem and the problems of the empirical sociologist. He reproaches even Montesquieu for not having gone back to the basic principles of law and for having been content to give a descriptive comparison of existing forms of law. But this is not the sense in which Rousseau understands the "spirit of the laws." In the first draft of the *Social Contract* he says: "There are a thousand ways of bringing men together; there is only one way of truly uniting them. Therefore in this work I give only one method for the formation of political societies, though there are perhaps no two among the variety of associations that at present exist which have arisen in the same way and not a single one which was formed in the way I have indicated. But I am seeking the rights and basis of society, and am not quarreling about facts." (Je cherche le droit et la raison et ne dispute pas des faits.)[44] But this disclaimer of Rousseau's did not prevent the historical school of jurisprudence from treating the social contract as an historical event, and as such from criticizing and repudiating it. Even today there is no agreement among Rousseau's critics on this point.[45] Rousseau's mode of expression does indeed lack full precision of statement here as elsewhere and admits of several interpretations.

But Kant could grasp his central thought in only one sense, and he elaborated this sense clearly and unequivocally. As in his critique of knowledge, in his philosophy of law he strictly divides the question of *quid juris* from that of *quid facti*. He regards the historical occurrence of the

[44] Vaughan, I, 462.
[45] Further details in Franz Haymann, *Jean Jacques Rousseaus Sozial-philosophie* (Leipzig, 1898), 57ff.

social contract not only as insignificant, but even as impossible; he argues, however, that its meaning is not thereby destroyed or even rendered questionable. In the *Metaphysical Basis of the Theory of Law* he declares that "the act through which a people constitutes itself a state, or to speak more properly the *idea* of such an act, in terms of which alone its legitimacy can be conceived, is the original contract by which all (*omnes et singuli*) the people surrender their outward freedom in order to resume it at once as members of a common entity, that is, the people regarded as the state (*universi*)."[46] Such a contract is thus "by no means to be necessarily assumed to be a fact—indeed it is not even possible as such"; it is "a mere idea of reason which has, however, its undoubted (practical) reality: that is, it obligates every lawgiver to promulgate his laws in such a way that they could have arisen from the united will of an entire people, and to regard every subject, in so far as he desires to be a citizen, as though he had joined in assenting to such a will. For that is the touchstone of the legitimacy of every public enactment."[47] Thus Kant achieved the same methodological transformation in the concept of the social contract as he had carried out in the interpretation of Rousseau's "state of nature." He transformed both from an "experience" into an "idea." He believed that he had thereby taken nothing from their value, but had in a strict sense grounded and secured this value.

IV. THE PROBLEM OF OPTIMISM

IN 1755 Voltaire delivered the first mighty blow at the system of philosophic optimism, in his poem on the Lisbon

[46] *Rechtslehre,* par. 47 (*Werke,* VII, 122).
[47] *Werke,* VI, 380f.

earthquake. Leibniz's arguments for the "best of all possible worlds" still retained their full force in the first half of the eighteenth century, and had become widely known through Pope's *Essay on Man*. But against Pope's dictum, "Whatever is is right," Voltaire now used the whole arsenal of his dialectic and rhetoric. He declared that only an abstract and remote philosophy which has put on blinkers to hide the suffering of existence could endorse such a thesis, and that it could be defended only with sophistical arguments:

> D'inutiles douleurs éternel entretien!
> Philosophes trompés qui criez: *"Tout est bien"*
> Accourez, contemplez ces ruines affreuses,
> Ces débris, ces lambeaux, ces cendres malheureuses,
> Ces femmes, ces enfants l'un sur l'autre entassés,
> Sous ces marbres rompus ces membres dispersés;
>
> .   .   .   .
>
> Direz-vous, C'est l'effet des éternelles lois
> Qui d'un Dieu libre et bon nécessitent le choix?
>
> .   .   .   .
>
> Non, ne présentez plus à mon coeur agité
> Ces immuables lois de la nécessité,
> Cette chaîne des corps, des esprits, et des mondes
> O rêves de savants! O chimères profondes!
> Dieu tient en main la chaîne, et n'est point enchaîné;
> Par son choix bienfaisant tout est déterminé,
> Il est libre, il est juste, il n'est point implacable.
> Pourquoi donc souffrons-nous sous un maître équitable?[48]

[48] And lamentations which inspire my strain,
Prove that philosophy is false and vain.
Approach in crowds, and meditate awhile
Yon shattered walls, and view each ruined pile,
Women and children heaped up mountain high,
Limbs crushed which under ponderous marble lie;

.   .   .   .

It is worthy of note that it should have been Rousseau, who never considered himself a *philosophe,* who accepted this challenge. He undertook the defence of Providence against Voltaire, as Leibniz had against Bayle. On August 18, 1756, he replied to Voltaire's poem in a letter in which he declared that it is not the function of a thinker to increase the ills from which mankind suffers by describing them in terrifying detail and thus condemning us to utter desperation. "The optimism you consider so horrible consoles me in the very misery you set forth as unbearable. Pope's poem assuages my pains and fills me with patience; yours increases my agony and forces me to protest against Providence; it takes all comfort from me and drives me to despair. In this strange contrast between what you prove and what I feel, I beg you to relieve my anxiety and to tell me where the deception lies, whether on the side of feeling or of reason." In these words Rousseau admits that his optimism is not the result of philosophic reflection and that to defend it he does not rely on logical argument. But he declares that it is so closely bound up with all he believes and so deeply rooted in his very nature that he could never renounce it without denying his own being. "All the

---

Say, will you then eternal laws maintain,
Which God to cruelties like these constrain?

.   .   .   .   .   .

Will you thus limit the eternal mind?

.   .   .   .   .   .

Allege not the unchanging laws of fate:
Urge not the links of the eternal chain,
'Tis false philosophy and wisdom vain.
The God who holds the chain can't be enchained;
By his blest will are all events ordained:
He's just, nor easily to wrath gives way;
Why suffer we beneath so mild a sway?
—*The Lisbon Earthquake*, W. G. Fleming tr., in *The Works of Voltaire* (Dumont, New York, 1901), xxxvi, 8ff.

subtleties of metaphysics would not lead me to doubt for a moment the immortality of my soul or a spiritual Providence; I feel it, I believe in it, I desire it, I hope for it and will defend it to my last breath."[49]

Like all the thinkers of the eighteenth century, Kant also experienced this inner conflict with regard to the problem of "theodicy"; he too had to travel a long road before he could take his stand with assurance on this question between the positions of Voltaire and Rousseau. In his description of the Lisbon earthquake, which appeared in 1756, he declared that "man is challenged to take thought by the awful visitations which affect his species, the convulsions of the very earth, the fury of the sea when shaken to its depths, mountains in fiery eruption," since they are "established by God as the rightful consequences of invariable laws."[50] Moreover, the *Essay on Some Considerations Concerning Optimism* which Kant published three years later still held to the position of the philosophic school of Leibniz and Wolff. Kant declares that one can maintain this to be "the best of all possible worlds" with a certainty that opponents can at least not contradict with any greater assurance. "If someone rises to assert that the highest Wisdom could have preferred the worse to the best, or that the All-Good could choose a lesser instead of a greater good equally in its power, I pay no further heed. It is a poor use of philosophy to employ it to undermine the principles of sound common sense, and we do it scant honor if, in order to frustrate such attempts, we find it necessary to take up the arms of philosophy."[51] But in his philosophic critiques Kant could no longer speak in this way. For he had himself declared the appeal to "common sense" to be invalid in metaphysical questions, and had

---

[49] *Correspondance Générale*, II, 324.   [50] *Werke*, I, 441.
[51] *Werke*, II, 35f.

refused to submit the judgments of "speculative reason" to the court of so-called "sound common sense."[52]

Thus Kant felt challenged to take up this problem anew, after he had rounded out his system, after completing the *Critique of Pure Reason,* the *Critique of Practical Reason,* and the *Critique of Judgment.* In 1791 he wrote a treatise to establish the *Failure of All Philosophic Attempts at Theodicy.* If speculative reason sets itself up as God's defender, he declares in this essay, it transcends the limits placed upon it. Its arguments cannot but turn into sophistry, and this results in making suspect the very cause it seeks to serve. Not only have all previous attempts at theodicy failed, but it can indeed be shown that they had to fail and will always have to. For it can be shown that our reason is altogether incapable of gaining insight into the relation between the world, however well we may know it through experience, and the highest Wisdom. The philosopher should not play the part of special pleader in this matter; he should not defend any cause whose justice he is incapable of grasping and which he cannot prove by means of the modes of thought peculiar to philosophy.[53]

Did Kant thus finally go over to the opposition? Did he decide against Rousseau and in favor of Voltaire? This question can be answered only if we keep in mind the transformation he effected in the way of putting the problem. If we mean by optimism that the totality of pleasure exceeds the totality of pain in the life of an individual or for mankind in general, Kant denies such a doctrine as emphatically and unambiguously as Voltaire or Schopenhauer. In the dispute between Rousseau and Voltaire a remark is quoted from Erasmus to the effect that few men could be found who would consent to be born again.[54] Kant

[52] *Werke,* IV, 7f.
[53] *Werke,* VI, 129ff.
[54] *Cor. Gén.,* II, 308.

took up this question and put it in an even more extreme form. "It is easy to decide," he says in the *Critique of Judgment,* "what value life holds for us, if its worth is measured merely by our enjoyments. . . . It is less than nothing; for who would wish to begin life anew under the same conditions or even according to a new self-made plan (but one consistent with the course of nature) that aimed merely at enjoyment?"[55] But Kant does not regard this as a denial of the value of life. For a new and different standard of value holds for him, the victor over the principle of eudemonism. The diminution of happiness can not lessen the value of existence, for this does not consist in what *happens* to a person, but in what a person *does.* Our deeds, not our outward fate, give life its meaning. For Kant this meaning cannot be impaired by any suffering, and no pessimistic argument can touch it. No matter how low we may estimate the value of human existence in terms of what man receives and enjoys, there remains the value that a free personality creates for itself. Only a good will can give man absolute value, and by reason of it the existence of the world can have a final purpose.[56]

Such a solution of the conflict between "optimism" and "pessimism," and such a transcending of the "dialectic of pure practical reason," of the opposition between happiness (*Glückseligkeit*) and being worthy of happiness (*Glückwürdigkeit*), was impossible for Rousseau. It would have required him to abandon the eudemonism at the basis of his ethical and religious views, for which he fought passionately. But for Kant the rejection of eudemonism definitely eliminates one aspect of Rousseau's thought. The chimera of a Golden Age and the idyll of a pastoral Arcady has disappeared. Man cannot and should not escape pain. For this

[55] *Critique of Judgment,* par. 83 (*Werke,* v, 514).
[56] *Critique of Judgment,* par. 86 (*Werke,* v, 522ff.).

is the spur to activity, "and in it we first feel our life; without it there would be lifelessness."[57] In all social life as well, it is only the opposition of forces, with all the suffering it entails for mankind, that at the same time makes possible the further operation of these forces. "Without it all excellent natural tendencies in mankind would forever lie dormant and undeveloped. Man desires concord, but nature knows better what is good for his species: nature desires discord. Man wants to live in ease and comfort; but nature aims to shake him out of his lethargy and passive satisfaction into toil and labor."[58]

Here is achieved a new and distinctive attitude toward life, unknown in this form either to Rousseau or to his opponents, Voltaire and the Encyclopedists. With regard to happiness, Kant recognizes only the attitude of complete renunciation. As his *Anthropology* declares, satisfaction in life is for man unobtainable; and even if there were such a thing we should not desire it, for it would mean stagnation and the blunting of all activity.[59] But Kant is just as far from seeing the meaning of human civilization in the over-refined satisfactions it provides. There was a period in which he had considerable respect for such satisfactions, and in his earlier writings, especially in his *Observations on the Feeling of the Beautiful and the Sublime,* we sense a delicate appreciation of all the charms of aesthetic cultivation and social intercourse. But as he grew older, Kant increasingly renounced them too. If he speaks of the value of life, we hear in him only the strict demands of his ethical rigorism. "Is not a righteous man still supported by the consciousness of having upheld and done honor to mankind in his own person, even in the greatest misfortunes of life, which he might have avoided if he could only

---

[57] *Anthropology,* par. 60 (*Werke,* VIII, 120ff.).
[58] *Werke,* IV, 156.   [59] *Werke,* VIII, 124.

have disregarded his duty? . . . This comfort is not happiness nor even the smallest part of it. For no one desires such an opportunity, nor perhaps even life itself under such circumstances. But he is alive and cannot bear to be in his own eyes unworthy of life. . . . He continues to live only because of a sense of duty, not because he has the slightest taste for life. . . . Duty's title to respect has nothing to do with happiness. It has its own peculiar law and its own peculiar tribunal. And no matter how one might wish to shake up duty and pleasure together in order to offer them as a medical compound, as it were, to an ailing spirit, they will presently separate out of their own accord, and if not, duty will not function. Even if in this way physical life gained a certain strength, the moral life would inevitably decline." [60]

Rousseau was destined by fate to the very syncretism Kant here condemns. He set up a strict and lofty ideal of virtue, but he demanded, as the price of serving it, the fulfillment of his yearning for happiness. Only then would he believe in a benevolent Providence guiding human destinies, and he postulates it for this purpose: "I feel it, I believe it, I desire it, I hope for it, I shall defend it to the last breath." Kant no longer believes that civilization, even in its highest perfection, can bring about the happiness of mankind, and he no longer asks it to. For him civilization has another law peculiar to itself. It is not the source of happiness, and its meaning does not even consist in providing men with intellectual satisfactions. It is rather the setting in which man is to test and prove his freedom. And he must undergo this test ever and again. Here the mature wisdom of Kant coincides with Goethe's: "He only earns his freedom and existence, who daily conquers them

[60] *Werke*, v, 97ff.

anew." In this conquest life achieves that meaning with which man alone can endow it, and this constitutes not his happiness but rather his distinctive dignity.

V. "RELIGION WITHIN THE LIMITS OF MERE REASON"

No aspect of Rousseau's philosophy has met with such different and conflicting interpretations as his theory of religion. It has been viewed from the most varied perspectives, and quite opposite judgments have been passed upon its content and value. All the efforts of modern research, all the critical analyses of Rousseau's work, have not dulled the edge of this contrast. During his life Rousseau passed as the uncompromising opponent of the Christian dogma, as the Deist, the enemy of the faith. As such he was exposed to the persecution of the ecclesiastical and political powers. After his death the judgment was reversed: men saw in him primarily the reviver of feeling, who in contrast to the reigning eighteenth-century devotion to reason rediscovered the distinctive meaning of religion and saved it from dissolution and destruction. But on this point also opinions as to the true content of Rousseau's faith have been in sharp disagreement. On the one hand men have seen in him the thinker who not only faithfully preserved the heritage of Protestantism, but founded it anew in a more profound and purely spiritual sense. On the other, men have claimed him for Catholicism, they have even tried to see in him the forerunner of the Catholic "Restoration" that began in the nineteenth century. The latter view is best represented in Masson's work on Rousseau's religion—the most comprehensive account that Rousseau's theory of religion has received. Masson's account is very penetrating, and thoroughly examines every single source for Rousseau's religious development. But that it fails to establish its central thesis, modern criticism, it seems to me, has proved with irrefutable arguments.[61]

Rousseau has been described equally as a strict rationalist and as a mystical enthusiast, while on the other hand critics have not been wanting who have tried to deny him any genuine religious sense at all. Thus Seillière sees in what Rousseau calls his religion only the morbid inflation of his own egotism, and a pathological deification of himself. "Jean-Jacques, direct reflection of God—that is Rousseau's religion."[62] We see that the estimate of Rousseau's religion has run through almost the whole scale from heaven to hell, from beatification to damnation.

In what sense is Rousseau himself to blame for this complete divergence of opinion? If we concentrate on the crucial document of his religious philosophy, if we plunge into the study of the *Profession de foi du Vicaire savoyard,* we shall hardly be inclined to make him responsible for all the ideas ascribed to him in the course of time by his interpreters. For the *Profession of Faith,* taken as a whole, possesses a great simplicity and clarity of intellectual structure. We never find in it those sudden transitions, those sharp paradoxes, those unreconciled contradictions that confront us in Rousseau's first writings. The whole work is inspired with genuine passion, but this passion is under control and expresses itself in clear and tranquil language. Rousseau is trying to convince, not merely to persuade; and his passion is never, as in the great peroration

[61] Masson, *La Religion de Jean Jacques Rousseau* (3 vols., Paris, 1916ff.). For criticism of Masson's work cf. Schinz, *La pensée religieuse de Jean Jacques Rousseau et ses récents interprètes,* Smith College Studies in Modern Languages, Vol. x, No. 1 (Paris, 1927) ; and G. Beaulavon, "La philosophie de J.-J. Rousseau et l'esprit cartésien," *Revue de Métaphysique et de Morale,* 62nd year (1937), 325-352.
[62] Ernest Seillière, *Jean-Jacques Rousseau* (Paris, 1921), 329.

of the first *Discourse*, purely rhetorical. It expresses an integrity of feeling and a consistency of thought.

Only one thing we can of course neither expect nor demand of Rousseau here. He does not analyze ideas precisely, and he never moves within the limits of a fixed philosophical terminology. Such a terminology he always felt as a fetter, which he indignantly cast off. He does not weigh his words; even as a writer he follows the impulse of the moment and seizes upon the expression that impulse suggests. Hence we must not take any of his expressions too strictly, and we must not press them if we are to do justice to his thought. In the *Profession of Faith* Rousseau tries to found religion now on "reason," now on "instinct"; he speaks of it as a "divine voice," and he derives it immediately from the "inner light"; he indicates as its foundation now "feeling," now "conscience." All these expressions may be hard to reconcile, and they open the door to a variety of interpretations. But a closer examination that is not bound by the letter leaves no doubt, it seems to me, that Rousseau's religious ideas are consistently thought out, and that they maintain a very definite direction from which they never stray.

Rousseau's religion aims above all at being a religion of freedom, and from this fact it draws its characteristic and crucial traits. In religion also Rousseau rejects any dependence on external authority and any subjection to it. This at once excludes tradition as a religious source. There is no traditional doctrine that can lead us by a royal road to God; we must seek the way ourselves, and traverse it alone. The principle of mere Scriptural authority is hence abandoned once and for all. The written word can never constitute the mediator between man and God, whatever sanctity we may ascribe to it. Instead of uniting it divides, and in the end it threatens to erect between us and the

Divine an insurmountable wall. The number of texts increases, commentaries are heaped upon commentaries: "How many men between God and myself!" Hence Rousseau dares not only to reject revelation as the foundation of religion, but to accuse it of being arbitrary and fortuitous; he speaks of the *"fantaisie des révélations,"* each of which makes God speak in accordance with its own ideas. Had mankind but listened always to God as he speaks in the heart of men, there would be on earth but a single religion.

But here a new objection arises. Can the heart really show us the way to that single and original natural religion that Rousseau is seeking and trying to teach? Is the heart not rather itself the most multifarious, changeable, and variegated thing in the world? If we follow the heart alone, are we not at the mercy of every breath of air? does not every new impression we submit to create a new self and with it a new God? This objection would be irrefutable, if as a religious philosopher Rousseau were not far from being the prophet of sentimentality, who considers every stimulus of feeling to be alike and who grants to each one free play. But he drew a clear and distinct line here himself. His religion of *"sentiment"* by no means intends to be a religion of "sentimentality." For here too the same criterion applies, the criterion of freedom. In mere feeling, in pleasure and pain, in the passions that sweep over man, man is determined from without; he feels himself subjected and delivered over to them. But there is a sphere in which this passivity stops short; and only there do we find that true self that is the bearer of religious feeling.

At this point Rousseau transcends the limitations of the sensationalistic psychology. The self is not a datum of sense and can never be understood as the mere product of sense data. It is an original activity, and the only evidence of such activity available to man. And this spontaneity of the self, not its receptivity, is the mark of the Divine. He who cannot think of himself as a free being is cut off from every approach to God. "No material being is active in itself, but I am. . . . My will is independent of my senses; I consent or I resist, I am defeated or I conquer. . . . I have always the power to will, not the force to execute. When I yield to temptation, I am acting under the compulsion of external objects. When I reproach myself for this weakness, I am listening only to my will; I am slave through my vices, and free through my remorse; my feeling of freedom is effaced only when I am depraved, and when I finally prevent the voice of my soul from raising itself against the law of the body." [63]

Can we label this confession of faith, as a critic of Rousseau has done, an "emotional Deism"? [64] This, it seems to me, would be possible and credible only if in describing religious experience Rousseau had confined himself to the expressions "feeling," "heart," "inner voice," "instinct." The history of religion and of religious mysticism makes clear how ambiguous all these expressions are and how very diverse forms of faith can lay claim to them. But in the end Rousseau himself summed up all these different aspects in one, and this is for him the real center of religious certainty. He closes his confession of faith with the appeal to conscience, and in it he finds the true source of religion. "Conscience! Conscience! divine instinct; immortal and heavenly voice; sure guide of a being ignorant and limited, but intelligent and free; infallible judge of good and evil, which makes man like unto God, it is thou who formest the excellence of his nature and the morality of

[63] *Profession,* 185.
[64] Cf. Babbitt, *Rousseau and Romanticism,* 122.

his actions; without thee I feel nothing in myself to raise me above the beasts, save the sad privilege of wandering from error to error with the aid of an understanding without rule and a reason without principle."[65]

Here is the core of Rousseau's religion, and what links it immediately to Kant. Not without reason have all the accounts of the Kantian moral philosophy placed the famous apostrophe to duty in the *Critique of Practical Reason* side by side with this passage from Rousseau's *Profession of Faith*. Rousseau like Kant is certain that the only road to a knowledge of God leads through the conscience, and that here lies the key to all religious truth. The only theology either can admit and recognize is ethical theology. Rousseau has likewise no need of any "theoretical" religion, if by the term we understand one that rests on strictly metaphysical proofs for the existence of God and the immortality of the soul. He distrusts all such proofs, and he declares that they are superfluous and even harmful for what is essential in the certainty of faith. To metaphysical dogmatism he opposes his "involuntary scepticism"; but at the same time he declares that this scepticism does not touch the heart of religious faith, for genuine religion contains not ideas for the understanding but precepts for action. "I seek to know only what concerns my conduct; as for dogmas which influence neither actions nor morality, with which so many people torment themselves, I never trouble myself about them."[66] In the same fashion Kant too had to "destroy knowledge in order to make room for faith"; he had to overthrow the dogmatic metaphysics of rational theology in order to be able to erect upon its ruins the edifice of his critical ethics. "My son," the Savoyard Vicar says in closing his profession of faith, "keep thy soul always in such a condition that it will want

[65] *Profession*, 273.   [66] *ibid.*, 416f.

God to exist, and thou wilt never doubt him. And whatever religion thou mayest profess, consider that the true duties of religion are independent of the institutions of men; that a just heart is the true temple of God . . . that there is no religion that absolves one from the duties of morality, and that these are the really essential things, that inner worship is the first of these duties, and that without faith there can be no true virtue."[67]

This is precisely Kant's "faith founded on practical reason." It makes ethical certainty the support and foundation of religious certainty, instead of basing the former on the latter. So far as I can see there is to be found in Rousseau's writings no evidence that on this central point he ever wavered. In this respect his religious ideas are far more consistent than those of Rousseau the anthropologist, the critic of culture, the philosopher of law and politics. "I do not like that mystical and figurative way of speaking," says Julie in the *New Héloise,* "which tries to nourish the heart with the chimeras of the imagination, and which puts mere feelings modeled on earthly love in the place of the true love of God. I leave aside the subtle interpretations of dogmas I do not understand; I cling to the shining truths that strike my eyes and convince my reason; to the practical truths that instruct me in my duties. . . . Is man master of what he believes or does not believe? is it a crime not to understand the art of demonstration? No, conscience tells us nothing of the truth of things, it gives us rather the rules for our duties; it does not prescribe what we have to think, but what we have to do; it does not teach us to reason correctly, but to do good. . . . Goodness, righteousness, morality, virtue: these are what Heaven demands and what it rewards; this is the true worship God demands of us."[68]

[67] *ibid.,* 441f.   [68] *New Héloise,* Bk. VI, letter 8 (IV, 270ff.).

This answers also the question of the "rationalism" of Rousseau's theory of religion. It is strange that in this connection any doubt ever arose, that in things of religion men could ever take him for an "irrationalist." The obstinate battle he fought against the "intellectuals," against the Encyclopedists, must not mislead us: it was intended not as a battle against reason but in its behalf. The profession of faith of the Savoyard Vicar remained firm in this conviction even in the midst of the conflict with the *philosophes*. The truest and most sublime ideas we can conceive of the Divine spring from reason itself, and from reason alone: "les plus grandes idées de la divinité nous viennent par la raison seule." No revelation can make reason unnecessary or take its place. For when revelation asks us to subordinate reason to faith, it must give us reasons for this subordination, and thus reinstate reason in its rights. The conflict with the *philosophes* was thus for Rousseau directed not against reason as such, but against the false use of reason. What he objected to in the *philosophes,* the thinkers of the *Encyclopedia,* was that they misunderstood and obscured the nature of the problem. They made thinking the measure of religious truth, instead of judging that truth by ethical certainty, which is alone possible. No wonder that in so doing they went astray, that in trying to fight dogmatism they themselves fell into dogmatism once more, though their dogmatism bore an opposite stamp. But reason must not be equated with mere ratiocination: "the art of reasoning is not reason, often it is the abuse of reason."[69]

To be sure, Rousseau still lacked the sure methodological weapon to carry through his fight. We can therefore understand why men charged him with an untenable mediating position, why the defenders of traditional faith—like its

[69] *Lettres Morales,* II (*Cor. Gén.,* III, 352).

opponents—regarded him as their irreconcilable enemy. He would have been spared the misunderstandings that here obtained if he had had a "critique of reason" at his command; if he could have rested his claim on that clear and certain line of demarcation that Kant, not without Rousseau's influence, laid down between theoretical and practical reason, between dogmatic and moral certainty.

And here we come to still another trait which, so far as I see, has never been adequately appreciated in the accounts and estimates of Rousseau's philosophy of religion, although it is of the greatest importance for the history of ideas. Rousseau as well as Kant put the ethical aspect so much in the center of religion that both almost lost sight of nature. Kant thought his critique had destroyed all previous attempts to mount from nature to God. He denied all validity to the "cosmological" proof of the existence of God as well as to the "physico-theological" proof. We cannot arrive at God by ascending in the series of causes and effects from the conditioned to the unconditioned, by regarding God as the First Cause and the Prime Mover. And the teleology of nature gives us just as little right to infer a highest Intelligence as its Author. Rousseau likewise gave up this form of proof of God, together with all other purely metaphysical arguments. But in his case this abandonment must at first glance seem highly paradoxical; for it excludes for him the possibility of finding any immediate bridge from nature to God. There is now no longer any direct transition; not nature but morality, not any knowledge of the objective order of the world, but only conscience can show us the way to God.

But how much more remarkable this consequence appears coming from Rousseau than from Kant! For had not Rousseau founded a new cult of nature, and did not the momentous influence he exercised rest on just this cult?

Had not the *Émile* become, in Goethe's words, the "Haupt-und Grundbuch" of this new gospel of nature?[70] When Rousseau added to this book his "profession of faith," and made it the core of the whole, we might have expected that this profession would be erected on a naturalistic foundation. But the opposite is the case. To be sure, Rousseau declares in the *Profession of Faith* that he had closed all books in order to read only in the book of nature.[71] And he repeatedly declares that he always felt disposed to worship God truly only when he stood in immediate contact with nature and hearkened to her language. Within the walls of cities and in the narrow precincts of a church, he says, his reverence could never attain its full strength. "I arose each morning before sunrise," he tells in describing his life at Les Charmettes, ". . . I climbed through a neighboring orchard on a beautiful path that led through the vineyard. . . . During the middle of my walk I offered up my prayer, which was not the idle stammering of the lips but a genuine elevation of the heart toward the Author of that friendly nature whose beauties lay before my eyes. I have never found any inclination to pray in my chamber; it seemed to me that the walls and all the petty work of men around me intruded between myself and God. I love to contemplate him in his works, while my heart is lifted to him."[72]

Thus it is Rousseau's feeling for nature that again and again became for him the source of religious feeling. But if the feeling for nature awakens and strengthens in him the feeling for religion, it does not enter immediately into its content. We might say of Rousseau's religion, with a Kantian turn, that the feeling for nature is its occasion but

---

[70] Goethe, *Dichtung und Wahrheit,* Bk. xiv (Weimar ed., xxviii, 254).
[71] *Profession of Faith,* 395.   [72] *Confessions,* vi, 19.

is nevertheless not its source. Any kind of mere deification of nature is alien to Rousseau. To appreciate this fact we must compare Rousseau with Shaftesbury. In his *Hymn to Nature* Shaftesbury turns immediately to the mighty "Genius of Nature." "O glorious Nature! supremely fair and sovereignly good! all-loving and all-lovely, all-divine! whose looks are so becoming and of such infinite grace; whose study brings such wisdom, and whose contemplation such delight. . . . O mighty Nature! wise substitute of Providence! impowered creatress. . . . Thy being is boundless, unsearchable, impenetrable. In thy immensity all thought is lost, fancy gives over its flight, and wearied imagination spends itself in vain, finding no coast nor limit of this ocean, nor, in the widest track through which it soars, one point yet nearer the circumference than the first centre whence it parted."[73]

This is genuine pantheism, which loses itself in the infinity of nature. But we find no such tones and no such dithyrambic exuberance in Rousseau's profession of faith. This profession, too, is filled with the strongest inner passion; but this passion points in another direction. The religion that Rousseau is teaching and proclaiming in the *Profession of Faith* does not arise from absorption in the wonders of nature, although the teleological argument retains for him its full force and he declares that it is just as absurd to assume that the world came into being without an intelligent cause as to assume that a work like the *Aeneid* could originate from throwing letters together by chance. But the real miracle that is central for him is the miracle of human freedom and of conscience as the evidence for this freedom. Here he finds the true mediator

[73] "The Moralists," iii; Anthony Earl of Shaftesbury, *Characteristics of Men, Manners, Opinions, Times, etc.*, ed. John M. Robertson (London, 1900), ii, 98.

between man and God. Shaftesbury gave to the work in which he included his *Hymn to Nature* the title of *"The Moralists."* But his own religion is not founded in the first instance upon morality. It is not an ethical but an aesthetic religion; it arises from the intuition of the beauty of the universe.

In erecting his philosophy Shaftesbury subordinated the good to the beautiful, and he tried to derive good from beauty. But this is as little Rousseau's course as it is Kant's. Rousseau is in earnest in his religious ideas with the "primacy of the practical." For him God is not only the Creator and Sustainer of nature, he is, to employ the Kantian phrase, "sovereign in the realm of ends." For Rousseau's religious philosophy is internally consistent with his philosophy of law and the state and is determined by their main ideas. For him religion is written in the hearts of men by the idea of justice, which he holds to be eternal and immutable, and not to be touched by the multiplicity and arbitrariness of positive laws. "No one," he writes to Vernes, "can reverence the gospel more sincerely than I; I consider it the most sublime of all books. . . . But in the end it is only a book, a book of which three quarters of mankind know nothing. Shall I believe that a Scythian or an African is less dear to our common Father than you and I, that he has deprived them rather than us of the means of knowing him? No, my friend, not in the few scattered pages of a book but in the hearts of men must we seek God's law. Here he has inscribed the precept: 'O man, whoever thou mayest be, turn within thyself, learn to consult thy conscience and thy natural faculties, then wilt thou be good, just, virtuous, bow before thy Lord and in his heaven share in eternal blessedness without end.'"[74] Rousseau speaks in the same way in the *Moral*

[74] To Vernes, March 25, 1758 (*Cor. Gén.,* III, 314f.).

Letters, which, since they were written for Mme. d'Houdetot and not intended for publication, give a particularly
intimate picture of his religious thought:[75] here too the
feeling of justice stands for him as the true title of nobility
which nature has inscribed in the hearts of men.[76]

VI. CONCLUSION

AT the close of our examination we take up again the
question from which we set out. What does the relation
between Rousseau and Kant have to teach us about the
connection that holds for both great thinkers between life
and philosophy? We have cited the words of Fichte:
"What kind of philosophy a man chooses depends upon
what kind of man he is." If these words are to mean that
it is the empirical individuality of the philosopher that
impresses its stamp on his ideas, and that it is therefore
futile to seek to understand these ideas before penetrating
into this individuality and in a certain sense becoming one
with it, then they are immediately contradicted by the results of our investigation. For between Rousseau and
Kant there could never exist such a form of mutual understanding, and no such "sympathy" could ever bind them
together.

As individuals they not only belonged to different hemi-
spheres of the *globus intellectualis;* to some extent they
formed its opposite poles. This holds for the forms of
their thinking as of their lives. What fellowship could
exist between Kant, the stern and reflective thinker, and a
man who in his autobiography himself confessed that he
was denied all power of cool thinking, that everything he

---

[75] On the content and character of these letters, cf. esp. C. W. Hendel, *Jean-Jacques Rousseau, Moralist* (Oxford, 1934), I, 298ff.

[76] *Cor. Gén.,* III, 364ff.

thought and wrote he could create only in the intoxication of passion?[77] Where could we find any conformity between the life of Rousseau, who was early filled with an unquenchable desire to wander and who declared that the happiest hours he had enjoyed had been those of his aimless tramping about—and the life of Kant, which kept within the narrowest bounds and seemed never to feel the desire to pass beyond them?

Rousseau was in a sense always fleeing from himself; and even in old age he remained the "lonely wanderer," as he described himself in one of his last works. Kant in contrast longed for nothing more than not to have to alter in any way or on any point the course he had entered upon. "I dread any change"—with these words he gave his reason for declining the call to Halle, in a letter to Markus Herz—"even though it appears very likely to better my condition, and I think I must respect this instinct of my nature. So I thank most heartily my patrons and friends who are so kindly disposed towards me as to concern themselves with my welfare; but at the same time I urgently request them to direct this disposition toward fending off . . . any disturbance of my present situation and preserving me in it."[78] This sensitive shrinking from anything new, unaccustomed and unforeseen determined also the external course of Kant's life and gradually fastened upon it more and more the shackles of a carefully considered plan. He became gradually more and more "the man of the clock."

What a contrast there is here too with Rousseau, to whom every external restriction was unbearable, and who in one of his dialogues has described the happy moment in which he resolved to throw away his watch, that it might not continually remind him of the time! "Thank

[77] *Confessions*, x, 473.   [78] *Werke*, ix, 174.

Heaven, I cried out in a passionate outburst of joy, now I shall no longer find it necessary to know what time of day it is."[79]

And yet all this, as we have seen, did not stand in the way of the fellowship of spirit between the intellectual world of Rousseau and that of Kant, which endured to the end. Such a fellowship would not indeed have been possible if the two had not been in contact at some more profound stratum of their beings. But this contact did not take place in anything arising from the mere "existence" of the two, from the circumstance of their lives or their way of judging the particular goods of life. Differently as they thought of these goods, they met in the definite demands they made on the world and on men. Divided in everything determined by the external circumstances of life, by profession and rank, by social milieu—divided also in personal peculiarities, in the manner and direction of their temperaments, Kant and Rousseau have a grasp on a definite idea which they both desire to establish and validate in an objective sense. They are both enthusiasts for the pure idea of right. Kant said that if right should be curtailed or destroyed man's existence on earth would lose all its meaning. Rousseau experienced the first violent shock to his being when he had to recognize that society, which should be the protector of right, had in all its previous forms become the tool of oppression and of the crassest injustice. In his first writings he sees no escape except a complete reversal and return; he demands that the *"homme des hommes"* transform himself once more into the *"homme de la nature."* But to this pure negation there succeeds the new positive construction he aims to complete in his political theory and his theory of education.

All this must have appealed to Kant immediately, and it

[79] *Rousseau juge de Jean-Jacques,* 2nd Dialogue.

must have all but extinguished for him the contrast he felt with the personality of Rousseau and his manner of "existence." Perhaps, too, he saw this contrast far less clearly than we see it today. In a sense it must be taken as a happy dispensation that Kant regarded Rousseau, although he was Rousseau's immediate contemporary, from a much greater distance than is for us today the case. He devoted himself without prejudice to the study of Rousseau's work, and he sought to recognize the man in the work. He saw in him the author of the *Discourse on Inequality,* the *Social Contract,* the *New Héloise,* not of the *Confessions,* which appeared only later when Kant's notion of Rousseau had long been fixed. But for us, who are familiar with all the details of Rousseau's life, who know his autobiographical writings, and his correspondence, and who are able to supplement them with contemporary sources, this wealth of information has often obscured the true knowledge of Rousseau's nature and work more than it has added to it. There are familiar writings in the Rousseau literature which give us in place of the work almost the man alone, and which describe him only in his dissensions and divisions, in his inner contradictions. The history of ideas threatens here to disappear into biography, and this in turn appears as a pure case history.[80] Kant possessed a much simpler and a consistent picture of Rousseau, which in just this simplicity was not less but more true than that which modern interpretation has often drawn for us.

But if Kant and Rousseau are united in a great common task, in the fulfillment of this task there fell to their lot quite different missions. Rousseau was first to see the goal,

[80] I am thinking here of such works as Seillière's *Jean-Jacques Rousseau* and Babbitt's *Rousseau and Romanticism.* The best and most informed refutation of this view is in my judgment to be found in the work of C. W. Hendel, *Jean-Jacques Rousseau, Moralist.*

and he proclaimed it with enthusiastic exuberance. He had to conquer strongly rooted prejudices and to clear away great obstacles. All this could hardly be accomplished by means of tranquil thinking. He had to call to his aid all the powers of passion, and to speak with the force of a new rhetoric. In him we encounter the first outburst which can control itself only with effort. Rousseau never learned to speak the language of "clear and distinct ideas." But Kant's thought was bound up with this language. He demanded definiteness and accuracy in ideas and clarity and perspicuity in their architectonic construction. He had to think Rousseau's ideas further, and he had to complete them and give them a systematic foundation. And in so doing it developed that this foundation led to a problem of absolutely universal significance, to a problem that included a genuine "revolution in men's way of thinking." Only through a critique of the entire "faculty of reason" could Kant solve the conflict that had inspired Rousseau in his fight against the *philosophes;* only in this way could he create that wider and deeper idea of "reason" which could do justice to Rousseau's ideas and incorporate them in itself.

SOURCES AND LITERATURE

The quotations from Kant's writings are taken from my collected edition of *Kants Werke* (11 volumes, Bruno Cassirer Verlag, Berlin, 1912ff.).

The *Fragmente aus Kant's Nachlass* are not contained in this edition; together with other notes of Kant they were to be collected in a separate volume, whose appearance was unfortunately prevented by the outbreak of the first world war. For these fragments reference is therefore made to Hartenstein's edition (*Immanuel Kants Sämtliche Werke,* in chronologischer Reihenfolge herausg. von G. Hartenstein, Bd. VIII, 609-645; Leipzig, 1868).

For the quotations from Rousseau's writings, since the texts in the familiar collected editions, especially in the older ones, are not always free from errors, I have tried to employ the best critical editions of the individual works. The following abbreviations are used:

P.W.   *The Political Writings of Jean Jacques Rousseau.* Edited from the original manuscripts and authentic editions. With introduction and notes. By C. E. Vaughan, 2 vols. (Cambridge, 1915).

Cor. Gén.   *Correspondance générale de Jean-Jacques Rousseau,* ed. Th. Dufour, 20 vols. (Paris, 1924-1934).

Nouv. Hél.   *La Nouvelle Héloïse,* ed. Daniel Mornet, Les Grands Ecrivains de la France, 4 vols. (Paris, 1925).

Confes.   *Les Confessions de J. J. Rousseau,* éd. intégrale publiée sur les manuscrits originaux par Ad. von Bever, 3 vols. (Paris, 1913).

Rêveries   *Les Rêveries du Promencur Solitaire,* ed. von Bever, *ibid.,* III, 189-338.

Prof.   *La Profession de Foi du Vicaire Savoyard.* Édition critique par Pierre Maurice Masson (Fribourg et Paris, 1914).

GOETHE AND THE KANTIAN PHILOSOPHY

IN GOETHE'S *Conversations with Eckermann* there occurs a curious remark, of great importance for his biography and for the history of ideas, which has scarcely been mentioned by students of Goethe, or at least has never been given the right interpretation. It deals with Goethe's relation to the Kantian philosophy.

"Kant," says Goethe, "never took any notice of me, although independently I was following a course similar to his. I wrote my *Metamorphosis of Plants* before I knew anything of Kant, and yet it is entirely in the spirit of his ideas."[1]

"Was ist mit diesem Rätselwort gemeint?"—"What means this riddle?" we are tempted to ask with Faust, in reading this passage. The words are indeed paradoxical. What has Goethe's *Metamorphosis of Plants* to do with Kant? And how could Goethe say that his conception of nature agreed with Kant's ideas? At first glance we can discover no similarity between them, we see only a sharp contrast. This contrast can be expressed in two words, "mathematics" and "Newton." Before becoming the critic of pure reason, Kant began with the study of Newtonian physics. His first major work, the *Allgemeine Naturgeschichte und Theorie des Himmels,* aimed to extend, complete, and generalize Newton's ideas. And in his metaphysics Kant never abandoned this course. "The true method of metaphysics," he declares, "is at bottom identical with that which Newton introduced into natural science, and which there led to such useful results." This

[1] Conversations with Eckermann, April 11, 1827 (*Gespräche*, III, 372). In this study Goethe's *Gespräche* are quoted from the edition of Flodoard Freiherr von Biedermann (5 vols., Leipzig, 1909ff.).

pronouncement still belongs to Kant's pre-critical period; it occurs in his paper for the prize competition of the Berlin Academy on clearness and distinctness, on evidence in the metaphysical sciences.[2] But Kant always maintained this position. The theory of nature was always for him the mathematical theory of nature. "I assert," he wrote as late as 1786, in the Preface to his *Metaphysische Anfangsgründe der Naturwissenschaft,* "that in any particular theory of nature we can find only so much of real science as we can find mathematics. . . . A pure physical theory of determinate natural objects is possible only through mathematics; and . . . hence any theory of nature will contain only so much of real science as it permits the application of mathematics."[3]

This is in sharpest conceivable contrast to Goethe's notion of nature. Goethe's theory of nature was one continued attack on Newton and Newtonian physics. During the course of his life this attack grew sharper and sharper, and it finally led to a tragic climax. Everywhere—among philosophers, physicists, biologists—he looked for allies in this contest, but he was able to convince scarcely anyone. Here he stood alone, and this isolation filled him with a growing bitterness. But what could *Kant* mean to him in this struggle, Kant the pupil and the philosophical interpreter of Newton, Kant, who had taken it as his aim to investigate critically the logical conditions of Newtonian science? Kant demanded that mathematics should enter into every part of the theory of nature, Goethe energetically rejected any such notion. "Physics must be divorced from mathematics," he said. "It must be completely independent, and try to penetrate with all its loving, reverent,

[2] *Kants Werke* (ed. Cassirer), II, 186.
[3] *Metaphysische Anfangsgründe der Naturwissenschaft, Werke* (ed. Cassirer), IV, 372.

pious force into nature and its holy life, quite regardless of what mathematics accomplishes and does. Mathematics, for its part, must declare itself independent of everything external, go its own distinctive and important way, and cultivate a greater purity than is possible when as heretofore it concerns itself with existence and endeavors to win something from it or to conform to it."[4]

From this it is clear that there was for Goethe no approach to Kant through physics. Nor could Kant the logician, the critic of pure reason, offer him any fundamental ideas. We know that in contrast to Herder he felt great admiration for Kant's masterpiece. He did not fail to make a real effort to understand it. His copy of the *Kritik der reinen Vernunft,* preserved in Weimar, shows the intensive study he devoted to it. But as a whole the work could never come to have for him the significance it held for Schiller. It grew out of another way of thinking—and it lay outside the course of his life and training. He felt this clearly himself. "It was the entrance," he said, "which I liked. I never dared to advance into the labyrinth itself; my poetic gifts or my common sense soon stopped me, and I never felt I was getting much out of it."[5]

Was it then only a compromise that led Goethe finally to acknowledge the Kantian philosophy—and was it his friendship with Schiller that forced him to this compromise? Historians of German literature have long maintained this position, and even today it seems the reigning opinion. But this view is untenable. It was not Schiller who opened Goethe's eyes to Kant. Long before his intimate association with Schiller he had found his way to

[4] Goethe, *Maximen und Reflexionen: Nach den Handschriften des Goethe und Schiller-Archivs* herausgegeben von Max Hecker (Schriften der Goethe-Gesellschaft, Bd. 21; Weimar, 1907), No. 573, p. 124.

[5] "Einwirkung der neueren Philosophie," *Naturwissenschaftliche Schriften* (Weimar ed.), II Abteilung, Bd. XI, 49.

Kant. On this point we possess conclusive evidence. As early as 1790 Koerner wrote to Schiller of a visit of Goethe's to Dresden: "Goethe was here a week, and I spent a good deal of time with him. I soon succeeded in getting closer to him and he was more communicative than I had expected. Where we found most points of contact you will hardly guess. Where else but—in Kant? In the *Kritik der Urteilskraft* he has found food for his philosophy."[6] It was the *Critique of Judgment* which was for Goethe the key to the understanding of the Kantian philosophy. And it was more than a philosophy—more than purely theoretical ideas—that he found in it. He has himself described for us clearly and precisely this first impression in his essay *Einwirkung der neueren Philosophie:* "But the *Critique of Judgment* fell into my hands, and to this book I owe one of the happiest periods of my life. Here I saw my most diverse interests brought together, artistic and natural production handled the same way; the power of aesthetic and teleological judgment mutually illuminated each other. . . .

"If my way of thinking was not always able to agree with the author's, if I seemed to miss something here and there, still the main ideas of the work were quite analogous to my previous production, action and thought. The inner life of art as of nature, their mutual working from within outward, were clearly expressed in the book. It maintained that the productions of these two infinite worlds exist for their own sake, and that things that stand beside each other do indeed exist for each other but not purposely on each other's account."[7]

In these last words we arrive at the real link between Kant and Goethe. The second part of the *Critique of Judgment* bears the title, "Critique of Teleological Judg-

---

[6] October 6, 1790.
[7] "Einwirkung der neueren Philosophie," *Naturwiss. Sch.,* XI, 50f.

ment." Even here Kant demands a clear line of demarcation. He by no means wishes to exclude the conception of "end" in considering biological phenomena. He declares that a purely mechanistic description of living processes is impossible. "It is quite certain that we can never get a sufficient knowledge of organized beings and their inner possibility, much less get an explanation of them, by looking merely to mechanical principles of nature. Indeed, so certain is it, that we may confidently assert that it is absurd for men even to entertain any thought of so doing, or to hope that maybe another Newton may some day arise, to make intelligible to us even the genesis of but a blade of grass from natural laws that no design has ordered. Such insight we must absolutely deny mankind."[8]

But although Kant not only recognized the concept of end as a heuristic principle for the investigation of nature, but even regarded it as quite unavoidable, though he called it a maxim of pure reason, he sharply rejected the previous naive and uncritical form of teleological explanation. In the eighteenth century the force of this type of explanation was still unbroken. This kind of thinking is familiar to the literary historian in a work like Brockes' *Irdisches Vergnügen in Gott*. Everything in nature serves the honor of God—but everything serves at the same time the ends of man; everything is arranged for him, for his use and advantage.

But what we smile at today in reading Brockes' book is by no means unique. Genuinely philosophic thinkers spoke just like Brockes—for instance, Christian Wolff, whom Kant called in the Preface to the second edition of the *Critique of Pure Reason* the "author of the not yet extinguished spirit of thoroughness in Germany." Even Wolff

[8] Kant, *Kritik der Urteilskraft*, par. 75 (*Werke*, ed. Cassirer, v, 478f.; tr. Meredith [Oxford, 1928], 54).

never draws a sharp line between teleology and mere utility. His German metaphysics, his *Vernünftige Gedanken von Gott, der Welt, und der Seele des Menschen, auch allen Dingen überhaupt,* Wolff followed up in 1726 with a separate work, *Vernünftige Gedanken von den Absichten der natürlichen Dinge.* As the title states, it is intended for "lovers of truth." But it is at bottom something rather different. It is no book for philosophers; it is really a manual for the German Philistine of the eighteenth century. Whenever he was in doubt about the purpose of any natural thing, he needed only reach for his Wolff to find at once the correct explanation. He is there enlightened about everything in the world, about sun, moon and stars, about air and winds, about vapors, mist, clouds, dew, frost, rain, snow and hail.

I am content to cite here some especially drastic examples. Why does the pole star exist? Wolff asks. "The pole star," runs the answer, "and the stars in general serve to tell us . . . our directions, which in particular proves exceedingly useful to travelers when they lose their way in the evening or at night; likewise to those whom night overtakes in the field or the woods, and who must follow their direction if they wish to find the way home."

How simple and how plausible, how informative and edifying! Or take a second example. What is the use of daylight? "Daylight . . . is of great use to us: for by daylight we can easily go about our duties, which we can either not perform at all at night, or at least not so easily, and at some expense, since it is necessary to make it light by art." The man speaking here is not the man who was with some justice called the *praeceptor Germaniae,* the teacher of Germany in the eighteenth century. Here we are listening only to a scholar of the cast of the apprentice Wagner —the honest and thrifty professor who sitting at his desk is glad of the sunlight because it saves him the expense of his desk lamp. But the professor is far-sighted and impartial. He knows very well that night brings its goods also. "In the first place, it has its obvious use, that men and animals who have become tired during the day can refresh themselves again through sleep. But it serves also for some pursuits that can not be carried on by day, like catching birds and fish."[9] Now we know why sun, moon and stars, why day and night exist! The stars, that we may find our way home, the day for work, the night for sleep, and for catching birds and fish!

Attacks on this Philistine wisdom were not lacking in the eighteenth century. Voltaire wrote his *Candide,* one of his most biting and delightful satires. How good it is, the philosopher in this book explains, that God created us with noses; how else should we be able to put on our glasses! Kant cited these words of Voltaire with approval in an essay in which he examined the so-called physico-theological proof.[10] But he did not stop with the satire. He gave a critical analysis of the concept of end, to determine its character and its limits. Goethe accepted this analysis without reservation. For in his judgment of the naive teleology of the popular philosophy of the eighteenth century he was from the start in complete agreement with Kant. In a conversation with Chancellor von Müller[11] he remarked that popular philosophy had always disgusted him; hence he had the more easily inclined toward Kant, who demolished it. In the *Xenien* of Goethe and Schiller there is a distich entitled *Der Teleolog:*

[9] Christian Wolff, *op. cit.,* 3rd ed. (Frankfort and Leipzig, 1737), 74, 92, 125.
[10] Kant, *Der einzig mögliche Beweisgrund zu einer Demonstration des Daseins Gottes* (1763; *Werke,* II, 138).
[11] *Goethes Gespräche,* III, 50.

Welche Verehrung verdient der Weltenschöpfer, der gnädig
Als er den Korkbaum schuf, gleich auch den Stöpsel erfand.[12]

For this kind of consideration of utility Goethe felt all
his life an unconquerable aversion. "It is an unbounded
service of our old Kant," he wrote in a letter to Zelter, "to
the world, and I may add to myself, that in his *Critique of
Judgment* he effectively placed art and nature side by side,
and granted both the right of acting in accordance with
great principles without purpose. Spinoza had earlier inspired me with a hatred for absurd final causes. Nature
and art are too great to aim at ends, and they don't need
to either. There are relations everywhere, and relations are
life."[18]

But we still stand at the very entrance and vestibule of
our examination. For what we are now considering is
only the negative side. We see what both Goethe and Kant
rejected—but not what they both affirmed, what united
them positively. This union was rooted in another and more
profound kinship between their views. I can here only attempt to sketch this relationship very briefly and in barest
outline. It was Goethe who first coined the word "morphology." This term has today become quite current; it
has entered into general scientific usage. But we forget
too easily what an important and crucial methodological
change it meant for the biology of the eighteenth century.
With Goethe's idea of "morphology," with his conception
of the "formation and transformation of organic natures,"
a new ideal of knowledge was created. A modern botanist,
Hansen, has said of Goethe's theory of metamorphosis

12 What reverence is due the world's Creator, who when
  Creating the cork tree graciously also invented the cork.
  —*The Teleologist*

13 To Zelter, January 29, 1830, *Briefe* (Weimar ed.), XLVI, 223.

that the period of botany beginning with Goethe is related to the preceding one as chemistry to alchemy.[14]

To put it briefly and clearly, Goethe completed the transition from the previous *generic* view to the modern *genetic* view of organic nature. The generic view of the plant world found its classic expression in Linnaeus' system of nature. It holds that we have understood nature when we have succeeded in arranging it in the pigeonholes of our concepts, dividing it into species and genera, into families, classes, and orders. But for Goethe such an enterprise was not enough. According to him, what we grasp in this way are only the products, not the process of life. And into this life process he wanted, not only as poet but also as scientist, to win an insight; in it he saw what was greatest and highest. Here he was thinking and judging like Mephisto in the apprentice scene:

> Wer will was Lebendigs erkennen und beschreiben
> Sucht erst den Geist heraus zu treiben,
> Dann hat er die Teile in seiner Hand,
> Fehlt leider! nur das geistige Band.
> "Encheiresin naturae" nennts die Chemie,
> Spottet ihrer selbst, und weiss nicht wie.[15]

Goethe was a great admirer of Linnaeus. There is a passage in his works in which he places Linnaeus beside Shakespeare and Spinoza in the history of his own inner development—surely the highest praise he could pay him.[16]

---

[14] Adolf Hansen, *Goethes Morphologie*, Giessen 1919.

[15] He who would study organic existence,
First drives out the soul with rigid persistence;
Then the parts in his hand he may hold and class,
But the spiritual link is lost, alas!
Encheiresin naturae, this Chemistry names,
Nor knows how herself she banters and blames!
　　　　　　　　　　　—*Faust*, Bayard Taylor tr., Modern

[16] *Naturwiss. Sch.*, VI, 390.　　　　Library, New York, p. 66.

"I must confess," he says, "that after Shakespeare and Spinoza Linnaeus had the greatest influence upon me—and just through the reaction he provoked in me." In the fine essay in which Goethe describes the history of his botanical studies he indicates the character of this reaction. "That I may be clear about those circumstances, think of me as a born poet, seeking to mold his words and his expressions immediately on the objects before him at any time, in order to do them some measure of justice. Such a poet was now to learn by heart a ready-made terminology, to have a certain number of words and epithets ready, so that when he encountered any form, making an apt selection he should know how to apply and order them into an appropriate description. Such a treatment always seemed to me like a kind of mosaic, in which you put one finished piece next to another, in order finally to produce out of a thousand individual pieces the semblance of a picture; and so in this sense I always found the demand to some extent repugnant."[17]

Here we can see clearly the kinship between Goethe and Kant. Goethe protested against the "rigid way of thinking" he found in the philosophy and biology of his time. "When I advanced my morphological ideas," he says in his *Campagne in Frankreich,* "I was sorry to observe that the rigid way of thinking: nothing can come to be except what already is, held possession of every mind."[18] He did not completely reject this way of thinking; in his morphological writings he even says that it is the easiest and most natural way, and that as such it had been transmitted from the seventeenth century to the eighteenth, and from the eighteenth to the nineteenth, and would continue to serve

[17] "Geschichte meines botanischen Studiums," *Naturwiss. Sch.,* VI, 116.
[18] *Campagne in Frankreich 1792* (Weimar ed., XXXIII, 196ff.).

usefully in its own fashion to represent reality clearly and distinctly. But he demanded that it be enlarged and deepened, as only the "ideal way of thinking" could do, which "reveals the eternal in the transitory." Of this ideal way of thinking he says that it alone is capable of elevating us to the point where common sense and philosophy come to agree.[19]

The armor of the "rigid way of thinking," which in Goethe's words "had quite befogged the century," Kant penetrated at two points. He accepted the Newtonian theory of nature and its explanation of phenomena in terms of forces acting at a distance. But he wanted not only to describe the being of matter, he wanted to understand its genesis. And so he was one of the first to offer a theory of the evolution of the material world from the original nebulae to its present form. He was the author of the theory we today call the Kant-Laplacian hypothesis.

In biology Kant went a step further. He clearly envisaged the task and the goal of a general theory of evolution. "This analogy of forms, which in all their differences seem to be produced in accordance with a common type, strengthens the suspicion that they have an actual kinship due to descent from a common parent. This we might trace in the gradual approximation of one animal species to another, from that in which the principle of ends seems best authenticated, namely from man, back to the polyp, and from this back even to mosses and lichens, and finally to the lowest perceivable stage of nature. Here we come to crude matter; and, from this, and the forces which it exerts in accordance with mechanical laws (laws resembling those by which it acts in the formation of crystals), seems to be developed the whole technique of nature, which, in the case of organized beings, is so incomprehensible to

[19] *Farbenlehre, Naturwiss. Sch.,* VII, 120.

us that we feel obliged to imagine a different principle for its explanation.

"Here the archaeologist of nature is at liberty to go back to the traces that remain of nature's earliest revolutions, and, appealing to all he knows of or can conjecture about its mechanism, to trace the genesis of that great family of living things (for it must be pictured as a family if there is to be any foundation for the consistently coherent affinity mentioned). He can suppose that the womb of mother earth, as it first emerged, like a huge animal, from its chaotic state, gave birth to creatures whose form displayed less finality, and that these again bore others which adapted themselves more perfectly to their native surroundings and their relations to each other; until this womb becoming rigid and ossified, restricted its birth to definite species incapable of further modification, and the multiplicity of forms was fixed as it had stood when the operation of that fruitful formative power had ceased. . . . An hypothesis of this kind may be called a daring venture on the part of reason; and there are probably few, even among the most acute scientists, to whose minds it has not sometimes occurred."[20]

Here Goethe could see himself and his own fundamental convictions. In his essay *Anschauende Urteilskraft* he described how deep a joy he felt when he first read this passage in the *Critique of Judgment*. "I had at first," he says, "found my way unconsciously and by an inner impulse to that primordial and archetypical origin, I had even succeeded in constructing a plausible sketch. Now there was nothing to prevent me any longer from resolutely embarking on the venture of reason, as the old man of Königsberg himself called it."[21]

[20] *Kritik der Urteilskraft,* par. 80 (*Werke,* v, 498; tr. Meredith, 78f.).
[21] "Anschauende Urteilskraft," *Naturwiss. Sch.,* XI, 55.

Goethe's morphology culminates in his theory of metamorphosis. The poetic expression of this theory Goethe set forth in two great didactic poems, *Die Metamorphose der Pflanzen* and *Die Metamorphose der Tiere*. The scientific foundation we must seek in his scientific works. I cannot here go into the particulars of this foundation. I am content to sketch briefly in a few significant examples the chief stages in the development of the theory in Goethe's own mind. At their head I place here that famous conversation with Schiller, which formed the beginning of a deeper intellectual association between them and laid a firm foundation for their future friendship. The report of this conversation is to be found in Goethe's sketch *Glückliches Ereignis*. Goethe and Schiller had attended a lecture at the Jena Scientific Society. By chance they left the meeting at the same time, and a conversation began about the lecture. "We arrived at his house, the conversation drew me in; there I vigorously expounded the metamorphosis of plants, and with many suggestive strokes of the pen let a symbolic plant arise before his eyes. He listened to and looked at everything with great interest, with decided power of comprehension; but when I ended he shook his head and said: 'That is not empirical, that is ideal' [*Das ist keine Erfahrung, das ist eine Idee*]. I was taken aback and somewhat vexed; for he had emphatically stated the point that divided us. . . . But I collected myself and replied: 'I am very glad that I have ideals without knowing it, and even see them with my eyes.'

"Schiller, who had much more of shrewdness and self-possession than I, and who also hoped to attract rather than to repel me for the sake of his *Horen*, which he was considering publishing, replied as a trained Kantian, and since my stiff-necked realism gave many an occasion for vigorous contradiction, we fought for a while and then con-

[73]

cluded a truce; neither could consider himself the victor, each thought himself invincible. Words like these made me most unhappy: 'How can there ever be an experience that conforms to an ideal? For the distinctive thing about an ideal is that no experience can ever agree with it.' If he considered what I called empirical to be ideal, there must exist something mediating between the two to relate them! But the first step had been taken. Schiller's powers of attraction were great, he fascinated all who approached him; I took part in his plans and promised to give him for the *Horen* many things I had kept unpublished; his wife, whom I had loved and treasured from her childhood on, contributed her share to the lasting understanding, all our mutual friends were glad, and so, through the great and perhaps never-to-be-settled controversy between object and subject, we sealed a pact which has endured without interruption and produced much good for us and for others."[22]

When we read today Goethe's report of his conversation with Schiller, it is not hard for us to clear up the misunderstanding between them. Goethe was convinced that with his theory of metamorphosis he had placed biology on a new, empirically verifiable and trustworthy foundation. When Schiller declared that the "original plant" [*Urpflanze*] was not empirical but ideal—this necessarily astonished Goethe—and wounded him. For it called into question the empirical and objective significance of his fundamental idea. But that was surely not Schiller's intention. He was speaking as a "trained Kantian." And in Kant's system an ideal is not, as with Plato, something opposed to experience—something lying outside it and elevated above it. It is rather a moment, a factor in the process of experience itself. It has no independent, isolated ontological existence; it is a regulative principle that is necessary for

[22] "Glückliches Ereignis," *Naturwiss. Sch.*, XI, 17ff.

the use of experience itself, completing it and giving it a systematic unity.

The relation in the Kantian system between ideal and experience, between constitutive conditions and regulative principles, between concepts of the understanding and concepts of reason, is very difficult and complicated. I cannot here go into the details of this complicated relation; that would lead us too far into the depths of the Kantian theory and involve us in the thorny Kantian terminology. We can here indicate only one point. Goethe himself later arrived at a position from which he could agree with Kant on this question also. In Italy, when he first conceived the idea of the original plant, he thought of it as something actual, as a concrete existence. He looked for it—and he was convinced that he would one day discover it—just as he had found confirmation for his theory of the intermaxillary bone in man on a walk at the Lido near Venice. Goethe has himself told us in his *Italienische Reise* how he went one morning to the public garden in Palermo to think over the plan of his poem on Nausicaa. "But at once another ghost that had been haunting me at this time seized me. Many plants that I had been used to see in tubs and pots, and for the greater part of the year only under glass, were growing here freely in the open air, and when they realize their form completely they are more intelligible to us. In the sight of so many forms both new and familiar, the old fancy occurred to me again: among this multitude could I not discover the original plant? . . . My good poetic resolution was disturbed; the garden of Alcinous had vanished, a world garden opened before me." [23]

Goethe later learned to think of the original plant in a different fashion. He no longer hoped to see it with his eyes and to grasp it with his hands. But the value of his

[23] *Italienische Reise,* 17. April 1787 (*Werke,* XXXI, 147f.).

theory did not seem to him to have diminished or to have been called into question on that account. Now he no longer took offense when the original plant was called ideal. He himself called it that, and he used another expression that is genuinely Goethean and profoundly significant. He called it a symbol. "The fundamental maxim of metamorphosis," says Goethe in a conversation with Chancellor von Müller in July 1830, "must not be interpreted too broadly; if we say it is rich and productive like an ideal, that is the best way to put it." And when he sent Zelter, in 1816, a new edition of the *Metamorphose der Pflanzen*, he advised him to take the work only symbolically, and "always to think in reading it of any other living thing that progressively develops of itself."[24]

Whether in this intellectual transformation which the theory of metamorphosis underwent during the course of the years Kantian influences played a role—whether the intimate association with Schiller and the memory of that first conversation with him had a part in it—we do not need to decide. On this matter there is not, so far as I know, any conclusive documentary evidence. But it seems at least very probable—especially since Kant's influence on Goethe in his old age grew stronger and stronger and is unmistakable. Goethe himself said to Eckermann that it had been of great significance for his life that Lessing and Winckelmann influenced him during his youth, Kant during his old age.[25] All that we know of the development of his philosophical, moral, and scientific views confirms this utterance.

Kant was able to exert this influence on Goethe because at bottom the two agreed about dogmatic metaphysics.

[24] To Zelter, October 14, 1816 (*Briefe*, XXVII, 199).
[25] Conversations with Eckermann, May 12, 1825 (*Gespräche*, III, 204).

Even Goethe's Spinozism did not stand in the way. For the influence of Spinoza on his thought and feeling was far more ethical than metaphysical. He has himself described in *Dichtung und Wahrheit* what he found in Spinoza. "Do not misunderstand me here," he says. "The closest ties link us to what is most opposite to ourselves. The all-harmonizing peace of Spinoza was in marked contrast to my own excited striving; his mathematical method was the opposite of my poetic way of feeling and expression, and just that orderly way of treatment which men judge unsuited to moral subjects made me his passionate disciple, his convinced admirer."[26]

But where men expected and demanded of Goethe a dogmatic adherence to some particular religious, theological or metaphysical system, he almost always refused, and often with great harshness. He came to a sharp break on this score with many of the friends of his youth, with men like Lavater or Fritz Jacobi. In 1786 Fritz Jacobi made one last attempt: he sent Goethe his newly-published book *Von den göttlichen Dingen und ihrer Offenbarung*. In acknowledging it Goethe did not conceal his dislike of anything dogmatic. "Your little book," he wrote, "I have read with interest but not with pleasure. You have much to envy!—house, land and Pempelfort, wealth and children, sisters and friends. . . . But God has punished you with metaphysics and set a thorn in your flesh, while he has blessed me with physics, that I may rejoice in the contemplation of his works, of which he has given me only a few for my own."[27]

This was always Goethe's attitude. He had no desire to lay bare the secret of life; he rejoiced in life's infinitely

---

[26] *Dichtung und Wahrheit*, Bk. XIV (Weimar ed., XXVIII, 289).
[27] *Briefe*, VII, 213f. Jacobi's estate was at Pempelfort, near Düsseldorf.

rich surface. It was enough for him to describe life in symbols. The original plant became one more such symbol for him. "The True, which is one with the Divine," writes Goethe in his *Versuch einer Witterungslehre*, "never permits itself to be known directly; we look upon it only in reflection, in example, symbol, in particular and related appearances; we become aware of it as incomprehensible life and still cannot renounce the desire to comprehend it."[28] Here is a point on which there was no conflict between the views of Goethe and Kant.

What Kant aimed to set forth in the *Critique of Pure Reason* was the limits of pure reason. He had to solve this problem by logical means. He spoke as an epistemologist, limiting knowledge to its own domain, to the field of possible experience and to the principles of morality. All this Goethe could accept without reservation. He declared to Eckermann that of all thinkers Kant had incontestably been of greatest use, since he laid down the limits which the human mind is capable of attaining, and did not touch on insoluble problems.[29] The same sense of human limitation was strong in Goethe; but he felt and spoke as an artist. He composed that magnificent ode to which he gave the title *Grenzen der Menschheit:*

> Denn mit Göttern
> Soll sich nicht messen
> Irgendein Mensch.
> Hebt er sich aufwärts
> Und berührt
> Mit dem Scheitel die Sterne,
> Nirgends haften dann
> Die unsichern Sohlen,

[28] *Naturwiss. Sch.,* XII, 74.
[29] Conversations with Eckermann, September 1, 1829 (*Gespräche,* IV, 163).

Und mit ihm spielen
Wolken und Winde.

. . . . .

Was unterscheidet
Götter von Menschen?
Dass viele Wellen
Vor jenen wandeln,
Ein ewiger Strom:
Uns hebt die Welle,
Verschlingt die Welle,
Und wir versinken.[80]

This is Goethe's sense of humility and limitation. But it never led him to become a pessimist. For the insight into the finitude of human existence is not identical with the idea of the nothingness of that existence. Similarly Kant, the critic of pure reason, never became a sceptic. "The first step in matters of pure reason," says Kant, "which marks its childhood, is dogmatic. The . . . second step is sceptical and gives evidence of the caution of a judgment grown

[80] For against Gods
Let no man ever
Measure himself.
If he exalts himself
And if he touches
Stars with his head-top,
Nowhere, then, can he find
A secure footing,
And clouds and wind
Make easy sport of him.

. . . .

What, then, distinguishes
Gods from all humans?
That waves innumerable
Before them billow
A stream eternal.
We are raised by the wave,
Overcome by the wave,
And sink beneath it.
                    —*Limits of Humanity*

[79]

shrewd through experience. But a third step is still necessary, which belongs only to the matured and manly judgment founded on firm maxims whose universality is as-
sured. . . . Through it not merely temporary checks, but the
very limits of reason, ignorance not merely about one point
or another, but in respect of all possible questions of a certain kind, is not only assumed but proved from first
principles."[81]

Such a "matured and manly judgment" Goethe possessed, especially in old age. "Our opinion," he said in an
essay on geology, "is that it well becomes man to assume
that there is something unknowable, but that he does not
have to set any limit to his inquiry."[82] According to
Goethe, the greatest happiness of the thinker is to have
inquired into what can be known and to revere in silence
what cannot be known.[83] Kant thought and felt likewise.
For him the key to the supersensible, to the "intelligible"
world lay not in the theoretical but in the practical reason.
But even of the categorical imperative he said that, while
we do not comprehend its practical and unconditioned
necessity, "we comprehend its incomprehensibility, which
is all that can fairly be asked of a philosophy which seeks
to extend its principles to the limits of human reason."[84]

In this conclusion Goethe and Kant could agree, despite
all the difference and contrast between their natures. What
makes the insight into this connection difficult for us is
the fact that we are here still inclined to think in certain
traditional and conventional terms. We see in Kant the
culmination of abstract theoretical reflection, while in
Goethe we see, to use Schiller's term, the type of the
"naive" poet and artist. But this formal contrast does not

[81] *Kritik der reinen Vernunft,* 2nd ed., 789 (*Werke,* III, 514).
[82] "Karl Wilhelm Nose," *Naturwiss. Sch.,* IX, 195.
[83] *Maximen und Reflexionen,* No. 1207, p. 250.
[84] Kant, *Grundlegung zur Metaphysik der Sitten* (*Werke,* IV, 324).

suffice here. Certainly as an artist Goethe was "naive." He says in *Dichtung und Wahrheit* that he had had to accustom himself from youth on to understand his poetry as a "pure gift of nature." This gift of nature he could not command at will; he had to allow it free rein. He could not follow the advice of the Theater Director in *Faust:* "Gebt ihr Euch einmal für Poeten, so kommandiert die Poesie!"[35] When he tried to he usually failed.

But in this sense Goethe the scientist was not "naive." To be sure, even as scientific inquirer he remained always the intuitive thinker. When the botanist Link tried to illustrate Goethe's theory of the metamorphosis of plants by means of an abstract mechanical model, he vigorously objected. "In such efforts," he declared, "only the last formless sublimated abstraction is left, and the subtlest organic life is joined to the completely formless and bloodless universal phenomena of nature."[36] For everything formless and without figure Goethe felt an inner aversion. The eye—as he said of himself—was the organ through which he possessed the world. Like the warder Lynkeus in *Faust,* he was *"zum Sehen geboren, zum Schauen bestellt."*[37] Wherever he could no longer look and see, he could no longer comprehend and understand. It was this which always kept him away from mathematics—especially from the modern form of analysis discovered by Leibniz and Newton.[38] "No one can be more afraid of numbers than I," Goethe once wrote to Zelter about a plan to substitute a numerical notation for the notes of music, "and I have always avoided and fled from any form of numerical symbolism . . . as something formless and

[35] "If you claim to be a poet, let poems appear at your command."
[36] *Naturwiss. Sch.,* VI, 262.
[37] "Born to see, appointed to look."
[38] See on this point my article, "Goethe und die mathematische Physik," *Idee und Gestalt,* 2nd ed. (1924), 33-80.

depressing."[39] "Numbers, like our poor words," he said
another time in a conversation with Riemer, "are only
attempts to seize and express phenomena, approaches forever inadequate."[40] In this sense Goethe understood and
conceived his theory of color. In it he aimed, as he wrote
Schiller, to include nothing but the world of the eye, which
contains only form and color. Thus "all reasoning is transformed into a kind of representation."[41] But if Goethe
opposed mere reasoning, he by no means opposed theory.
"The highest wisdom," he says, "would be to understand
that every fact is already theory."[42]

Goethe recognized no sharp boundary between intuition
and theory; for such a boundary would have contradicted
his own experience as scientific investigator. For him the
two realms were not separated. The Foreword to the
Theory of Color already expresses this idea. "Merely looking at a thing," says Goethe here, "can tell us nothing.
Each look leads to an inspection, each inspection to a
reflection, each reflection to a synthesis; and hence we can
say that in every attentive glance at the world we are already theorizing."[43]

This is not "naive" at all; it rather expresses the clearest
insight of Goethe the scientist into the mutual relations of
phenomena and theory, of "idea" and "experience." "Time
is ruled by the swings of the pendulum, the moral and
scientific world by the oscillation between idea and experience."[44] By virtue of this attitude Goethe opposed what
he called "formless abstraction"; but to the spirit of analysis as he found it at its keenest and highest power in Kant's

[39] To Zelter, December 12, 1812 (*Briefe*, XXIII, 197).
[40] Conversation with Riemer, March 27, 1814 (*Gespräche*, II, 223).
[41] To Schiller, November 15, 1796 (*Briefe*, XI, 264).
[42] *Maximen und Reflexionen*, No. 575, p. 125.
[43] *Naturwiss. Sch.*, I, xii.
[44] *Naturwiss. Sch.*, VI, 354.

Critique he had no need to object. "We may each of us . . . say," he wrote in his remarks on that noteworthy session of the Paris Academy of 1830, in which the controversy between Cuvier and Geoffroy de Saint-Hilaire broke out, "that analysis and synthesis are two inseparable acts of living. . . . The more vigorously these functions of the mind cooperate, like inhaling and exhaling, the better will science and its friends be taken care of." [45]

Kant as critic of reason investigated the logical form, the principles of empirical knowledge; Goethe, as artist and as scientist, spoke of "ultimate phenomena" [*Urphänom-enen*]. In these ultimate phenomena he found the limit —a limit not only to thought, but also to vision. He asked the scientist not to transcend this limit—"to allow the ultimate phenomena to remain in their eternal peace and splendor." [46] "If the physicist can arrive at the knowledge of what we have called an ultimate phenomenon," says Goethe in the *Farbenlehre*, [47] "he is secure, and the philosopher with him. The scientist, for he is convinced that he has arrived at the limits of his science, that he is on that empirical height from which, looking backward, he can survey experience in all its stages, and looking forward, see into the realm of theory, even if he cannot enter it. The philosopher is secure; for he takes from the hand of the physicist an ultimate datum which becomes his starting-point." That this implies a certain renunciation, Goethe is clear. But this renunciation did not deter him. He saw in it a necessary theoretical demand, as he recognized it in practice as a moral command. "When I finally rest in the ultimate phenomenon," he says, "it is but resignation; but it makes a great difference whether I am resigned at the

[45] "Principes de Philosophie Zoologique," *Naturwiss. Sch.,* VII, 188.
[46] *Farbenlehre, Naturwiss. Sch.,* I, 73.
[47] *ibid.,* I, 287.

limits of man's reason, or within a hypothetical limitation of my restricted individuality."[48]

Goethe's view of art was not the same as Kant's, although he here felt himself very close to the Kantian theory, as Schiller mediated and interpreted it for him. But here too he sought far more for unity, while Kant was seeking for difference. Goethe was certain that the power of thinking like that of poetry is innate. And even in scientific inquiry he emphasized the necessity of imagination no less than that of analytic understanding. "At bottom a truly great scientist is quite unthinkable without this high power," said Goethe to Eckermann.[49]

> Wird der Poet nur geboren? Der Philosoph wird's
>   nicht minder,
> Alle Wahrheit zuletzt wird nur gebildet, geschaut.

This distich in the *Xenien* of Goethe and Schiller is entitled *Wissenschaftliches Genie*.[50] Here Goethe was departing from Kant's theory. For Kant had restricted genius to art, denying it to science. For Kant science has other sources; it rests on experience, observation, mathematical deduction, not upon intuition. Genius is the talent (a natural endowment) which prescribes rules to art. It cannot be learned, nor is it teachable. In contrast, every scientific proposition must have its fixed place in a definite system; it must be objectively grounded and demonstrable. This requirement marks science off from art. "In science the greatest discoverer is distinguished from the laborious imitator and disciple only in degree, while he is set off in kind from the man whom nature has endowed for fine

---

[48] *Maximen und Reflexionen*, No. 577, p. 125.
[49] To Eckermann, January 27, 1830 (*Gespräche*).
[50] *Xenien*, Weimar ed., Bd. v, Abt. 1, p. 213.

> Is none but the poet born? The same applies to the thinker.
> All truth, in the end, is merely molded, beheld.

art."[51] For Kant there are a priori principles of taste, as there are a priori principles of theoretical knowledge. Nevertheless nature and art, truth and beauty, remain divorced; they cannot be reduced to one and the same denominator.

For Goethe, on the other hand, there is no sharp division between the two domains. His motto remains the words of Shaftesbury: "All Beauty is Truth." For him the beautiful is "a manifestation of secret natural laws, which without its appearance would have remained forever hidden from our view."[52] Laws of nature and laws of beauty cannot be set off from each other in their origin or their meaning. The transition from the consideration of nature to the consideration of art is accomplished almost insensibly in Goethe's mind. He constantly alternates between the two and finds satisfaction only in this alternation. For the interpretation of nature of which Bacon had spoken must for him be always at once both theoretical and aesthetic. "He for whom nature begins to reveal her open secret," he says, "feels an irresistible longing for her most worthy interpreter, art."[53]

Kant's position in the intellectual history of the eighteenth century forms a difficult and complicated problem. The influences he received and those which extended from him have been as yet by no means completely investigated and comprehensively set forth. We are accustomed to picture Kant as the lonely thinker, the philosophical investigator, who, immersed and entangled in his own problems, paid little attention to the outside world and the events of his time. But this traditional picture is by no means accurate; on essential points it stands in need of amplification

[51] Kant, *Kritik der Urteilskraft*, par. 47 (*Werke*, v, 384).
[52] *Maximen und Reflexionen*, No. 183, p. 32.
[53] *ibid.*, No. 201, p. 35.

and correction. What passionate interest Kant took in the events of the French Revolution we know from the reports of his contemporaries. The deep influence Rousseau exerted on his intellectual development our preceding study has attempted to illuminate. It is true that Kant's outer life was that of the closet scholar, that he never left the walls of his native city. But that by no means prevented him from following the intellectual movements of his time with sharp eyes. None of them seem to have lain wholly outside the sphere of his vision. Herder, who during the 'sixties was Kant's pupil in Königsberg, has drawn for us a living and characteristic picture of his philosophical teaching at that time. From it we see that this teaching was by no means restricted to abstract problems, to questions of logic and metaphysics. It extended just as much to the fundamental questions of natural science, to psychology and anthropology, and it made full use of contemporary literature.[54]

To be sure, this interest was essentially restricted to Kant's pre-critical period. In the most productive period of his life, in the twelve years of preparation for his *Critique of Pure Reason,* it slowly ebbed away. Kant's acquaintance with the German literature of the eighteenth century stopped with Wieland. He seems to have known Goethe only as the author of *Werther.* But in that first period, which was just as much a period of receptivity as of productivity, and in which the two powers still preserved a balance, Kant received many stimuli which continued to act and which did not become philosophically fruitful in him until much later. The English literature on the idea of genius he followed and studied closely. In Germany Lessing had been the first to take up the fight against the younger generation, against the literary representatives of the ideals of the "period of genius." "We have now even a

[54] See Herder's *Briefe zur Beförderung der Humanität,* 79th *Brief.*

race of critics," writes Lessing in the *Literaturbriefe,* with
an allusion to Gerstenberg, "whose best criticism consists
in rendering all criticism suspect. Genius! Genius! they
cry. Genius transcends all rules!... 'Rules suppress genius.'
As though genius could be suppressed by anything in the
world—and besides, by something which, as they themselves confess, is derived from it. . . . Genius bears in
itself the touchstone of all the rules. It understands and
follows only those which express its own feelings in words.
And this feeling expressed in words, we are told, can
diminish its activity!" [55]

What Lessing here expresses in the form of an *apercu*
Kant brought into rigorously systematic form in the
Critique of Judgment, and sought to demonstrate through
an analysis of the judgment of taste and its meaning and
validity. For him too "fine art" is the art of genius. But
genius is by no means without rules or restraint in the
sense of the *Storm and Stressers.* It is rather the origin
and source of all genuine rules; it is "the talent or the innate disposition (*ingenium*) through which nature gives
rules to art." [56] In this definition of Kant's Goethe saw a
significant change not only in the history of philosophy,
but also in the general history of ideas. In *Dichtung und
Wahrheit* Goethe aimed not only to describe his own life
and to make clear for himself and others his own poetic
development. He aimed to give at the same time a history
of the entire intellectual and artistic culture of his time. In
this history he attributed to Kant a significant, indeed a
crucial position. He sees in his ideas the critical solution
of the old conflict between "genius" and "rules," which had
dominated the whole poetics of the eighteenth century and
left its stamp upon it. "The word genius," Goethe says of

[55] Lessing, *Briefe die neuere Litteratur betreffend,* Pt. I, 19th *Brief.*
[56] *Kritik der Urteilskraft,* par. 46 (*Werke,* v, 382).

his own youth, speaking of the period of *Storm and Stress,* "became a universal watch-word. . . . It was long before the time when it could be said that genius is that power of man which gives laws and rules through acting and doing. In those days it manifested itself only when it broke existing laws, overthrew established rules, and declared itself untrammeled. . . . And so I found an almost greater obstacle to developing and expressing myself in the false cooperation of those who agreed with me than in the opposition of those who disagreed. . . . The word genius was exposed to such misinterpretation that men thought it necessary to ban it completely from the German tongue. And thus the Germans, with whom what is base finds in general far more opportunity to spread than with other nations, would have lost the finest flower of speech, the word which only seems foreign, but really belongs to all peoples alike, if the sense for the highest and best, newly re-established by a more profound philosophy, had not fortunately been restored again."[57]

This is perhaps the finest appreciation of Kant's critical philosophy to be found in Goethe's works. It is all the more significant, in that the Kantian philosophy was able to offer him personally far less than it had given Schiller. For Schiller it had been the study of the Kantian philosophy that brought to a close the tumult of his youth. Only through this study was he able to overcome the period of *Storm and Stress*—to develop from the poet of *Die Räuber* and *Don Carlos* into the poet of *Wallenstein.* Kant's theory became for him a great disciplining force. It gave him intellectual security and moral maturity. In Goethe's life neither Kant's philosophy nor any other played such a role. He was always dependent upon his natural poetic powers; they early filled and formed his existence. "I had

[57] *Dichtung und Wahrheit,* Pt. IV, Bk. 19 (*Werke,* XXIX, 146ff.).

rescued myself," he writes in *Dichtung und Wahrheit,* of the first version of *Werther,* "more by this composition than by any other, from a stormy element which had tossed me forcibly to and fro, through my own fault and that of others, through accident and choice, through intention and haste, through stiff-neckedness and weakness. I felt as after a general confession, happy and free again, and entitled to a new life."[58]

It was the will to form, and the power of poetic form, which from the beginning distinguished Goethe from his youthful companions, from poets like Lenz or Bürger. What he had found in his own poetry he later sought in the works of nature and in the works of the ancients. They stood for him on the same level; for he found in them the same inviolable consistency and necessity. "The consistency of nature," he once wrote, "well consoles us for the inconsistency of men."[59] The same impression he derived from that vision of antiquity he had found in Italy. "These noble works of art," he says, "were produced by men as at the same time the highest works of nature, in accordance with true and natural laws; everything that is arbitrary and conceited falls away; there is necessity, there is God."[60]

When Goethe returned from Italy, when he again entered the sphere of his earlier life and work, he found even with his closest friends but little understanding and sympathy for all he had worked out for himself. He stood almost alone; he felt himself isolated and misunderstood. "From the forms of Italy," he says, "I had returned to formless Germany, exchanging a bright sky for a gloomy one; my friends, instead of consoling me and drawing

[58] *Dichtung und Wahrheit,* Bk. 13 (*Werke,* XXVIII, 225).

[59] Letter to Knebel, April 2, 1785 (*Briefe,* VII, 36).

[60] *Italienische Reise:* second stay in Rome, September 6, 1787 (*Werke,* XXXII, 77f.).

me to them again, brought me to desperation. My delight in the most distant and little known objects, my passion, my laments over what I had lost seemed to insult them, I met with no sympathy, no one understood my language."[61]

In this mood Schiller must have seemed to him to stand at the very antipodes. He found in him the representative of everything he had abandoned and thought he had overcome in himself. He saw in Schiller "a powerful but immature talent," who "had poured out upon Germany in rapturous streams" precisely "those ethical and theatrical paradoxes" from which Goethe had sought to purify himself.[62] It was many years before Goethe could master this feeling. All Schiller's wooing of his friendship he rejected coldly and harshly. Then suddenly came the reaction. The day arrived on which he no longer saw in Schiller the antagonist but the ally. Here too the Kantian philosophy played a noteworthy if only a mediate role. The "Kantian" Schiller, the author of the *Aesthetische Briefe*, Goethe could understand and respect. For here he found his own experience confirmed in a quite different medium. Goethe's classicism rested upon his idea of "inner form." This form he found in the works of the ancients, whom he saw in the light of Winckelmann's artistic views. It was for him the expression of an objective necessity. "There is nothing beautiful in nature," he says, "which is not motivated as true by natural laws."[63]

Schiller's path was different. He developed his aesthetic theory out of the Kantian concept of freedom: beauty meant for him "freedom in appearances."[64] But Goethe and Schiller could agree completely in the conclusion: since

[61] *Naturwiss. Sch.*, VI, 132.
[62] See on this point the essay "Glückliches Ereignis," *Naturwiss. Sch.*, XI, 14.
[63] To Eckermann, June 5, 1826 (*Gespräche*).
[64] See Schiller's correspondence with Koerner during 1793.

for neither did "freedom" and "necessity" mean mutually exclusive opposites. They found between the two ideas a relation of correlation, not of opposition. This correlation Kant had revealed in the moral realm, explaining that ethical freedom is identical with "autonomy," with self-imposed law. The classicism of Goethe and Schiller carried this view into art: it was rooted in the principle that only law can give us freedom. Here for both the circle of the "subjective" and the "objective" was closed. "The law appearing in phenomena produces, in the greatest freedom and in accordance with its own conditions, the objectively beautiful, which must indeed find worthy subjects to grasp it."[65]

In the recognition of universal and necessary natural laws Kant and Goethe are completely at one. But their ways of establishing and justifying this basic assumption are quite different. Kant follows his logico-analytic path. He begins with the analysis of the principle of causality, which he has to defend against the Humean doubt. He shows that if we make room for this doubt, experience would be transformed into a mere "rhapsody of perceptions."[66] But experience is in reality something quite different, and far more than that. It is no aggregate of sense-impressions, but a system. Such a system must rest on objectively valid and necessary principles. "Experience is possible only through the representation of a necessary connection between perceptions."[67]

This construing of the concept of nature follows for Kant from his conception and definition of the understanding. The understanding is for him the "faculty of rules";

[65] Goethe, *Maximen und Reflexionen*, No. 1346, p, 279.
[66] Kant, *Prolegomena zu einer jeden künftigen Metaphysik*, par. 26 (*Werke*, IV, 59ff.).
[67] *Kritik der reinen Vernunft*, 2nd ed., 218 (*Werke*, III, 166).

and the empirical rules of nature are only particular instances and applications of the a priori rules of the understanding. In this way the special laws of nature become "specifications of universal laws of the understanding." "We must . . . distinguish empirical laws of nature, which always presuppose particular perceptions, from the pure or universal laws of nature, which without being based on particular perceptions merely contain the conditions of their necessary union in experience; and in respect of these universal laws nature and possible experience are one and the same. . . . It sounds indeed strange at first, but it is nonetheless certain, when I say: the understanding does not derive its laws (a priori) from nature, but prescribes them to nature."[68]

Such an absolutely ruling and legislative understanding Goethe did not recognize. Here too he is unwilling to stop with mere thinking and judging; he is compelled to see. Kant declares that nature is "the existence of things, in so far as it is determined in accordance with universal laws."[69] Goethe cannot stop with such a nature, *"natura naturata"*; as artist and as scientist he desires to penetrate into *"natura naturans."* The idea of metamorphosis becomes his guide in this great process of the inner productivity of nature. Goethe does not think like Kant in terms of mere relations; he can think only in intuitive forms.

He begins by immersing himself in the fullness and multiplicity of the plant and animal world. But for him this fullness is not everything. In it he senses something different and more profound. "The particular," Goethe declares, "can not be the model for the whole. . . . Classes, genera, species and individuals are related as instances to

[68] *Prolegomena zu einer jeden künftigen Metaphysik*, par. 36 (*Werke*, IV, 72).

[69] *Prolegomena*, par. 14 (*Werke*, IV, 44).

a law; they are contained in it, but they do not contain or reveal it."[70] Even if we consider the implications of the form only in general, we should conclude without closer experience that living creatures very similar to each other must be produced by identical formative principles. While Kant looks for synthetic principles, for the highest principles of human knowledge, Goethe is looking for the productive principles of creative nature.

> Freudig war, vor vielen Jahren,
> Eifrig so der Geist bestrebt,
> Zu erforschen, zu erfahren,
> Wie Natur im Schaffen lebt.
> Und es ist das ewig Eine,
> Das sich vielfach offenbart:
> Klein das Grosse, gross das Kleine,
> Alles nach der eignen Art;
> Immer wechselnd, fest sich haltend,
> Nah und fern und fern und nah,
> So gestaltend, umgestaltend,
> Zum Erstaunen bin ich da.[71]

Just as Kant aimed to keep human knowledge close to experience and to limit it to the "conditions of possible

[70] Goethe, "Entwurf einer vergleichenden Anatomie," *Naturwiss. Sch.*, VIII, 73.

[71] Goethe, *Gedichte* (*Werke*, III, 84).

> Years ago with joy abounding,
> Eagerly the spirit sought
> To discover, to experience
> Nature living as it wrought.
> And it is the One Eternal,
> Self-revealing, manifold;
> Small is great and great is small,
> Each in its distinctive mold.
> Ever changing, still remaining,
> Near and far, and far and near;
> So in forming all transforming—
> Thus to wonder am I here.
>
> —*Parabasis*

experience," Goethe drew the same conclusion for vision and poetry. Here once more he found an unexpected confirmation of his own urge. As poet he had neither the power nor the desire to produce anything that did not arise out of his own experience. Poetic content, he declared, is the content of one's own life. "In my poetry I have never been untrue to myself," Goethe said to Eckermann. "What I did not live and what did not urgently demand expression and creation I have never composed or uttered."[72] In this sense there was for Goethe no difference between "poetry" and "truth"; and even the traditional opposition between "idealism" and "realism" he did not recognize as binding. "The spirit of the actual," he says, "is the true ideal"; and his imagination he declared to be an "imagination for the truth of the real."[73]

What we have here is a very strange analogy to Kant's way of thinking and philosophy. Kant was always the philosopher of the a priori. But for him a priori knowledge disclosed no distinctive and independent realm beyond experience. The a priori is rather a moment in the structure of empirical knowledge itself; it is bound to experience in its significance and use. Goethe felt strongly attracted by this conception of the "ideal": in his copy of the *Critique of Pure Reason* he underlined twice the passage in which Kant declares that everything the understanding derives from itself without borrowing from experience, it possesses for no other purpose than empirical use.[74]

The conclusion of Kant's transcendental analytic can be stated after a fashion in a single proposition. It is the proposition that concepts without content are empty. But

[72] Conversations with Eckermann, March 14, 1830.
[73] Conversations with Riemer, 1827; and with Eckermann, December 25, 1825.
[74] *Kritik der reinen Vernunft*, 2nd ed., 295 (*Werke*, III, 212).

according to Kant our concepts can receive a content only by being related to intuition—pure or empirical intuition. Without this relation we should indeed have forms of thought; but these forms would possess no objective meaning, no empirical value as knowledge. "Intuition and concept thus constitute the elements of all our knowledge, so that neither concepts without an intuition corresponding in some fashion to them, nor intuition without concepts, can give knowledge."[75] The pure concepts of the understanding are in themselves nothing but logical functions of judgment. If these functions are to pass from mere concepts into knowledge, they must be filled with intuition. "If the concept could be given no corresponding intuition, it would be a notion in its form, but without any object, and through it no knowledge at all of anything whatever would be possible; because there would and could be nothing to which my notion could be applied."[76]

From the outset Goethe must have felt strongly attracted by this theory. He here stood to Kant in a far freer relation than German academic philosophy. For the latter saw in Kant's thesis only the negative side, not the positive. To the pupils of Wolff and the adherents of the Wolffian ontology Kant was always the "Alleszermalmer," as Mendelssohn called him. For he had declared that the principles of pure understanding were "mere principles for the exposition of phenomena," and that therefore the proud name of an ontology which presumed to give in a systematic doctrine synthetic knowledge a priori of things in general, must give place to the modest name of a mere analysis of pure understanding.[77] In contrast, Goethe saw in this Kantian critique of academic philosophy not a work of

[75] *Kritik der reinen Vernunft*, 2nd ed., 74 (*Werke*, III, 79).
[76] *ibid.*, 146 (*Werke*, III, 123).
[77] *ibid.*, 303 (*Werke*, III, 217).

destruction but a work of liberation. He found here the main tendency of his own "objective thinking," which aimed not to abandon intuitions but to immerse itself in them.[78] And the Kantian modesty was also quite congenial to his thought. He was satisfied with the "colored reflection," and was convinced that in this colored reflection we possess life itself. "We live amidst derivative phenomena," he says, "and do not know how to arrive at the ultimate question."[79] This negation of "absolute" knowledge meant therefore no loss to him, and it set no determinate limits to his way of inquiry. "Of the Absolute in any theoretical sense," he declares, "I do not dare to speak; but I may assert that he who has recognized it in the appearance and always kept it in mind will experience great gain from it."[80]

Was the idea Goethe formed of the Kantian theory adequate? Can we grant it objective historical truth? This question can hardly be answered with a simple yes or no. I should certainly advise no one to adopt Goethe's conception and account of the Kantian philosophy in a textbook on the history of philosophy. Goethe himself has told us that when he occasionally became involved in conversation about the Kantian philosophy and advanced his own idea of it, the Kantians present would shake their heads. "It happened more than once that one or another confessed with smiling surprise: it was to be sure an analogue of the Kantian position, but a strange one."[81] More than such an analogue we may not seek in Goethe. He belonged to no philosophical school, and he swore by the words of no master. Here we must think of Goethe's Tame Xenion:

[78] See *Naturwiss. Sch.*, XI, 58.
[79] *Maximen und Reflexionen*, No. 1208, p. 251.
[80] *ibid.*, No. 216, p. 47.
[81] *Naturwiss. Sch.*, XI, 51f.

[96]

Was willst du, dass von deiner Gesinnung
Man dir nach ins Ewige sende?
Er gehörte zu keiner Innung,
Blieb Liebhaber bis ans Ende.[82]

In philosophy too Goethe remained the amateur. We can call him neither a Kantian nor a Spinozist in the strict sense of the words. But we need not on that account reject the inner truth of either his idea of Kant or his idea of Spinoza. Only we must then understand and define the concept of truth in his own sense. "What is fruitful alone is true," says Goethe. And Spinoza as well as Kant was eminently fruitful in him. Much that Goethe said about Kant is peculiar to himself, yes, unique. But precisely in this individuality it is significant and illuminating. "If I know my relation to myself and to the external world," says Goethe, "I call that truth. And thus every man can have his own truth, and yet truth is still one."[83]

In this sense we can understand and appreciate how the great artists of the classical period formed in their minds different ideas of Kant. In the essay *Winckelmann und sein Jahrhundert*—one of the finest characterizations of the eighteenth century—Goethe says that no scholar was able to reject with impunity the great philosophical movement begun by Kant, to oppose it, or to despise it.[84] This holds not only for the scholars but also for the artists. Very few of them remained wholly untouched by Kantian ideas. But each of them saw Kant in a new and different light and in his own perspective. Profound philosophical ideas

---

[82] *Werke*, III, 243.

    What would'st thou?—that into eternity
    Thy disposition one after thee send?
    He belonged to no profession
    Was an amateur right to the end.

[83] *Maximen und Reflexionen*, No. 198, p. 35.
[84] "Winckelmann und sein Jahrhundert," *Werke*, XLVI, 55.

work not only in their own circle. They become sources of intellectual light, which send out their beams in all directions. But what becomes of these beams depends not only on the character of the source of light, but also on the mirror they encounter and by which they are reflected. The manner of this reflection was different for Schiller, for Goethe, for Beethoven. For Schiller the study of the *Critique of Pure Reason* and the *Critique of Aesthetic Judgment* was guiding and crucial. Goethe came to Kant by way of the *Critique of Teleological Judgment*; Beethoven was seized and carried away by the *Critique of Practical Reason*. They all read the same Kant—and yet for each of them he was new and different, because he stimulated and made effective in them different productive forces, forces of an intellectual, moral, and artistic character.

SOURCES AND LITERATURE

THE quotations from Kant's writings are taken from my collected edition of *Kants Werke* (11 volumes, Bruno Cassirer Verlag, Berlin, 1912ff.). The quotations from Goethe are taken from the great Weimar edition. I have used for the *Gespräche mit Eckermann* the edition of Flodoard Freiherr von Biedermann (5 vols., Leipzig, 1909ff.). Goethe's *Maximen und Reflexionen* were edited from the manuscripts of the Goethe und Schiller-Archiv by Max Hecker (Schriften der Goethe-Gesellschaft, Bd. 21; Weimar, 1907).